8 · 24 · 71

HOW WILL WE MOVE ALL THE PEOPLE?
Transportation for Tomorrow's World

Today the problem of transportation has reached the crisis point. Traffic jams, polluted air, strangled cities and blighted suburbs are among the symptoms of this growing technological dilemma. Keyed to the current climate of awareness and ecological concern, this far-ranging book describes the wonders ready to leap from the drawing board to the assembly line to answer society's urgent needs.

TOMORROW'S WORLD SERIES

CLEAN AIR—CLEAN WATER FOR
  TOMORROW'S WORLD

HOW WILL WE MOVE ALL THE PEOPLE?
Transportation for Tomorrow's World

HOW WILL WE MOVE ALL THE PEOPLE?

Transportation for Tomorrow's World

by STERLING McLEOD
and the editors of
SCIENCE BOOK ASSOCIATES

with photographs

JULIAN MESSNER NEW YORK

Published by Julian Messner
a division of Simon & Schuster, Inc.
1 West 39th Street, New York, N.Y. 10018
All Rights Reserved

Printed in the United States of America

ISBN 0-671-32379-2 Cloth Trade
        0-671-32380-6 MCE

Library of Congress Catalog Card No. 74-139088

1609173

WE WISH TO THANK the many organizations in government, education and private industry whose assistance has made possible this look at transportation in tomorrow's world.

For their help in giving us access to files and reports, and for time generously spent in consultation, we are particularly grateful to many persons associated with the following governmental and educational research institutions:

California Institute of Technology, Carnegie Institute of Technology, Cornell Aeronautical Laboratory, the Environmental Science Services Administration, the Federal Aviation Administration, Massachusetts Institute of Technology, the Mellon Institute, the National Aeronautics and Space Administration, the National Air Pollution Control Administration, the Port of New York Authority, the Port Authority of Allegheny County, Pa., Rensselaer Polytechnic Institute, the University of Pittsburgh, Stanford Research Institute, the Urban Mass Transportation Administration, the U.S. Atomic Energy Commission and the U.S. Department of Transportation.

The Editors
Science Book Associates

CONTENTS

Rapid Transit
for the Millions

Rapid-transit trains that never stop, yet let passengers off at every station, wheelless vehicles that skim along above the ground at 300 miles an hour, trains that roll silently through 4,000-foot-deep tunnels at jet-airplane speeds: these are some of the developments that can help solve our most pressing transportation problem— the need to move large numbers of people swiftly and safely through the urban sprawl in which most of our population now lives. Exploding suburbs, traffic-choked freeways, fouled air and overflowing parking lots make that need a truly desperate one.

In many U.S. cities which have some kind of mass transportation, the systems are outmoded, little changed for half a century. With few exceptions, the railroads which once adequately connected major cities with their suburbs either are at the point of breaking down or have stopped running altogether.

Bumper to bumper traffic on city streets and freeways is not an efficient way to move millions of people!

Most American cities have no rapid-transit systems at all. In fact, in 1970 the Department of Transportation reported that 45 major cities depended entirely on helter-skelter bus systems and the automobile.

No one thinks that the kind of flexible, personal transportation provided by the individually owned car will ever disappear from the American way of life. Quite the contrary. Transportation experts are certain that the number of cars will continue to increase. However, they believe that if we use the technological opportunities available to us, we can lessen our dependence on the automobile. We will solve many problems, they say, if people, instead of driving to work, can turn to reliable, fast public transit systems.

In addition to reducing the traffic problems of big cities, rapid-transit systems can meet an important social need. They will make it possible for the inhabitants of the poorer areas of the cities to reach the suburbs. Increasingly, industry is moving to industrial parks on the fringes of metropolitan areas. The U.S. Department of Housing and Urban Development terms adequate transportation a "tragically missing link" between the cities' disadvantaged and the jobs that await them in the suburbs. In California, the Governor's Commission studying the Los Angeles riots discovered that it could take a citizen of the Watts area two hours and four transfers to get to an aircraft plant in Burbank by bus.

The personnel manager of a large construction company employing thousands of workers tells how the absence of public transportation affects the welfare of urban dwellers:

"Our company has a lot of construction projects going on in suburban areas and near cities, and often we are desperately short of help. A few miles from each project is a low-income area populated by men and women who desperately want jobs. We and they can't get together because there is no way that is quick enough and cheap enough for them to get to where we are. A city with a really good transit system, cheap and embracing the whole metropolitan area, might depopulate its ghettos in a couple of years."

Public reaction today is strongly against mass transit systems. Surveys show that people think of them as being noisy, dirty, crowded, undependable and slow. Indeed, many mass transit systems of today warrant those criticisms. What can we do to provide rapid transit that people will be eager to ride because it is quiet, clean, uncrowded, dependable and fast? Fortunately, science and technology have some practical answers.

Later we will take a look at some of the revolutionary transportation methods that are at the drawing-board or test stage, such as gravity vacuum transit and tracked air-cushion vehicles, which promise to create an exciting new era in tomorrow's world. But before they become realities there is much we can do to transform existing transportation systems—by automating them. What automation can accomplish is demonstrated by the world's first fully automated transportation system. BART—Bay Area Rapid Transit—is a 78-mile network that can move 100,000 people an hour into and through the Oakland–San Francisco area. Its gleaming trains can travel at speeds of 80 miles an hour, just 90 seconds apart, with complete safety.

BART is made possible by an electronic motorman, called a speed-distance regulator, which rides in the head car of the electrically operated train. There it receives messages from wayside transmitters—electronic devices that monitor each train as it passes—and from devices on the other trains. The computer interprets the messages it receives and operates the

12

Trains like this provide swift transportation for riders on BART (Bay Area Rapid Transit), the world's first fully automated system.

d. It automatically keeps
from any train ahead, and

his kind of automation is
a particular train get to
conds or minutes earlier.
of the line to carry more
engers a system can carry
which the trains run but
can travel.
. Holmes, a mass transit
y is expressed in the num-
be carried in an hour, and
of factors. To understand

13

this, it is helpful to think first about the line capacity of an escalator. If it is running more quickly, it will obviously carry more passengers in any given time than a slower escalator.

"But there comes a time, as the speed is increased, when passengers do not step on close together, and only alternate steps are occupied as the escalator moves up. At this speed, about 150 feet per minute, the capacity of the escalator falls suddenly. Each passenger reaches the top more quickly, but if there is a crowd waiting to go up, most of them will be delayed.

"In the same way, if passengers are allowed to walk up an escalator, they space themselves out farther apart and, though individual passengers make a quicker journey, the capacity of the escalator is reduced and it is carrying fewer persons per minute or per hour.

"In the same manner, if the speed of trains is increased, they must, for safety, travel farther apart. One may have fewer faster trains or more trains traveling more slowly, but there is one particular speed and number of trains which will give the maximum line capacity."

A future triumph for automation could come in the form of a train that lets its passengers off without stopping. This system is based on a car which is divided in half, lengthwise. The two sections, hooked together, run on parallel tracks. The main section, the part which keeps on going, is a regular subway car. The

14

other half is a seatless compartment, or corridor, that does the stopping.

When the combined train nears a station, the passengers who plan to get off step into the corridor section through doors which automatically open and then close again. At an appropriate point this corridor section separates from the coach section and comes to a stop at the station, while the main part keeps moving without any reduction of its speed. It is soon joined by a similar corridor section carrying passengers who got on it at the station just passed.

Thus, with the aid of automated controls, a mass transit system could be made to give faster service and convenience for passengers by making every stop an express stop. In an ordinary subway system, such as New York's, the average speed of express trains is only 20 miles an hour. That could be speeded up by the split-train system to 40 miles an hour, possibly higher. In New York a single line can carry about 36,000 passengers an hour at its peak. The split-train system could double that. While not yet in use, this nonstop train, developed by French engineers, is being studied by transit authorities the world over.

Automation can even be used to transform the commonplace bus into a high-speed, mass-transit vehicle. This has already been demonstrated by the Skybus, which rolls along what looks like an ordinary concrete highway. Actually, it is the Transit Expressway, an experimental, two-mile-long roadway outside Pitts-

Le Metro in Montreal shows what can be done with a modern subway system. Semi-automated trains move silently on rubber tires.

A lightweight steel car designed for new mass transit systems provides comfort for passengers.

*This Transit Expressway system operating outside Pittsburgh
is a pioneering venture in automated transportation.*

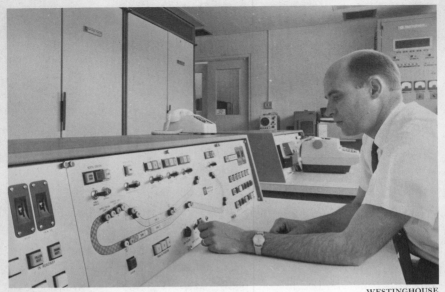

A single dispatcher sitting in a control room like this can monitor the performance of an automated Transit Expressway system.

burgh, and what you don't see is the system of wires and electronic apparatus housed in channels alongside it.

Step aboard the Skybus and you find yourself in a 34-foot-long vehicle rather like an ordinary bus. The first thing that will impress you, however, is the fact that there is no driver. His place has been taken by a set of electronic controls. A central computer keeps watch on the entire operation and on the speed, location and functioning of each car in the system. This computer sends messages to wayside controllers—actually small, specialized computers at each station. These controllers make split-second computations, based on the electronic data they themselves collect, and send directions to the buses via a wire which runs along the roadway.

Once a Skybus has stopped, the controllers signal the vehicle to open its doors. The car cannot move again until after all passengers have finished boarding and leaving the bus and its doors have closed. Sensors constantly monitor every phase of the Transit Expressway's operation. If this pulse taking hints at the slightest problem, a signal is sent to the computer control panel so that the dispatcher there can take corrective action. As part of this diagnostic feature, a high-speed electric typewriter can provide a printed report on the performance of the system every two seconds. The tiniest deviation from perfect operation, such as a fault in the air-conditioning equipment, can thus be detected promptly.

Any trouble along the route causes control mechanisms to brake the vehicle to an emergency stop. To keep the passengers from being puzzled or worried, a system is provided that permits the dispatcher at the central station to speak to the passengers over a loudspeaker. The sound of a human voice, designers say, is reassuring, particularly since most people, to begin with, are somewhat uneasy about riding on anything that doesn't have a motorman at the controls.

This is one of the problems designers of automated transportation systems must cope with. Assurances that the electronic monitors are far more capable than human beings to meet with all situations is not enough.

In the modern subway systems, such as the Montreal Metro, the motorman really has little to do, but he is nevertheless conspicuously present in the glassed-in compartment at the head of the train.

Automation can also play a role in fast ground transportation between cities that are relatively close to each other. In addition to the Boston–New York–Washington "Northeast Corridor," the Department of Transportation lists a number of other corridors which, its studies indicate, are in need of such systems of transportation:

Pittsburgh–Cleveland
Cleveland–Akron–Columbus–Cincinnati

Chicago–Detroit
Chicago–Minneapolis–St. Paul
Chicago–St. Louis
Washington–Atlanta
Jacksonville–Miami
Tallahassee–Mobile–New Orleans
Houston–San Antonio
Seattle–Portland
San Diego–Los Angeles–San Francisco

At present the only fast way of traveling between many of these cities is by air—a process that often necessitates trips to distant airports at each end. Highways through the urban sprawl around the cities are congested, and rail service either has been discontinued or functions so badly that travelers avoid using it. Still, the transportation planners argue, these cities are connected by railroad rights of way. Is there any way to upgrade these routes to meet the need for fast transportation?

U.S. engineers know that there is because exactly this problem has been faced and solved in Japan, where the "fastest railroad in the world," the Tokaido line, achieves speeds greater than 130 miles an hour as it flashes along the corridor between Tokyo and Osaka.

This rail system is a marvel of automation, controlled by computers in the Automatic Train Control Center in Tokyo. The linkage of computers with radio

21

The high-speed Tokaido trains, running between Tokyo and Osaka, have shown the advantages of fast trains on inter-city corridor runs.

and electronic sensors in tracks, trains and stations provides constant monitoring of the entire system. While there is an engineer aboard each train, his work consists mainly of braking the train as it comes into a station. Even this can be done automatically from Tokyo. The watchful monitoring equipment at headquarters not only keeps track of the speed and positions of trains but also considers such factors as the velocity of the winds buffeting them.

The success of the Tokaido Express has not been rivaled in the United States, but two new trains running on the Northeast Corridor have proved that fast interurban rail transport is no idle dream. In 1969 the Turbo Train started operating between New York and Boston. This sleek, streamlined, turbine-operated train can travel at 125 miles an hour, although unfortunately the tracks over which it runs do not permit such speeds.

The Metro Liner can go even faster, but, like the Turbo Train, it is kept from reaching anything like its 180-mile-an-hour capacity on the New York–Washington run, where it is in service.

Hampered as they are by inadequate trackage, these two trains show the potential for faster service on railroads not unlike those of today. They prove that faster, safer corridor transportation does not necessarily have to await the development of radically new, far-out systems.

PENN CENTRAL RAILROAD

The Metro Liner is a high-speed train that can run on existent roadbeds to speed up travel in corridors like that between New York and Washington, D.C.

The Turbo-Train achieves speeds of 125 miles an hour on ordinary twin rails. The cars have a special suspension system that prevents sway on curves.

Air Cushion Vehicles

The story of ground transportation has been the story of wheels. Carts, chariots, wagons, carriages, trains, cars, trucks—all have moved on the round marvels that are one of man's most fundamental inventions.

In tomorrow's world, wheels are going to be challenged by wheelless vehicles that may solve the intercity rapid-transit problem. In a huge proving ground near Pueblo, Colorado, you can see prototypes of these experimental TACVs—Tracked Air-Cushion Vehicles. They may not be exactly like the ones you may be riding in the late 1970s, but they give a hint of what is to come.

As they whoosh around a 20-mile oval track, their red and white paint jobs flashing in the bright western sunlight, they reach speeds of 250 miles an hour. Perhaps later models may go as high as 350, but this is fast enough to demonstrate the potential of vehicles that move not on wheels but on cushions of air.

The story of this form of high-speed, wheelless

transportation began in the early days of airplanes. Aerodynamic engineers noticed that when an airplane was on the ground, moving slowly or even standing still with its propeller turning, an updraft of air pushed on the wings. They soon determined that it was caused by the flow of air created by the propeller. Moving around the bottom of the plane, the air hit the ground and bounced upwards.

For a long time this "ground effect" was thought of simply as a nuisance. Engineers took it into consideration and designed planes so they would not be thrown off balance by it when taxiing. Then, in 1928, an American scientist, Dr. Arnold A. Kucher, was struck by a bold idea. Maybe this bouncing air could be put to work. Perhaps a vehicle could be made that would ride on a film of air instead of on wheels!

Kucher worked out a design that called for a platformlike hollow vehicle flared out at the bottom. Through an opening in the platform he proposed to force air downward at high pressure. It would, he theorized, provide lift that would get the platform off the ground. It was a basically sound idea, and some scale models did actually work; but compact engines that could produce a powerful enough air current were not available at the time. It would have taken such a large engine to create enough air to fill the chamber under the vehicle that it could not have operated efficiently.

The next big advance that made the air-cushion ve-

hicle practical came in the kitchen of a British aeronautical engineer, Christopher Cockerell. One day in
1951, Cockerell, who had long been fascinated by
Kucher's idea, got one of his own. Perhaps the flaw in
the Kucher design lay in that big open chamber into
which the air was fed. What if he covered the bottom
of the hollow chamber with a plate, leaving room for a
narrow jet of air to escape around the edges of the
plate? Or possibly he could put holes in the plate so
that many jets of air would escape from them.

It was such a simple concept that Cockerell was able
to try it out at once. For his first experiments he
headed for the kitchen, where he found a coffee can. In
its bottom he punched some holes. Then he thrust a
hair drier through a larger hole he cut in the top of
the can.

When he turned on the hair drier above the kitchen
table, the can lifted slightly off the table top. It was
floating!

Of course, much further experimentation was called
for, and many refinements in design were made after
the first crude coffee-can venture. In later experimental vehicles, various ways of designing the nozzles and
air ducts were found to deliver the air with greater
force. A major discovery was that a flexible rubber
skirt around the bottom confined the air somewhat and
still further increased the lifting effect. Whereas vehicles without the skirt were limited to getting only a

few inches above the ground or water surface, with the skirt they could rise many feet.

Cockerell's discoveries opened up a new world for the ground-effect machine, or air-cushion vehicle. Cockerell himself had visions of automobiles that could move without roads, trains that could run without tracks and ships that could ride above the highest waves. Researchers in many parts of the world went to work to develop versions of all three types of vehicles.

The first to come into practical use as a full-fledged means of transportation was the Hovercraft ferry that plies the English Channel. The huge air-cushion ve-

This giant air-cushion ferry, operating in the English Channel, is a forerunner of ocean liners that will move across tomorrow's seaways on cushions of air.

hicle, which made its maiden voyage in 1968, is 130 feet long and 70 feet wide, and comfortably carries 254 passengers and 30 cars. It makes the crossing in 35 minutes, compared with 90 minutes for a surface boat.

The start of a Hovercraft trip across the Channel is swift and smooth. The black neoprene skirt around the vessel balloons out when the propellers are turned on, and the craft lifts off the ground. Since it need overcome only inertia and air resistance, it quickly picks up speed. In minutes it is traveling at 70 miles an hour. In trials over smooth water, the big craft has gone 84 miles an hour. Passengers can look out the windows at the crests of waves that in the past often made Channel crossings a horror for queasy stomachs. The Hovercraft sails smoothly above them, without sway, pitch or roll.

What would happen if the air source should fail? Nothing that would injure or even shake up the passengers. As repeated test crashes have shown, the craft simply drops into the water with a mighty splash, but little rocking. And, of course, once on the water it floats in perfect safety, as seaworthy as any ship.

Air-cushion vehicles are certain to play an important role as ferries and short-haul boats. Their use is increasing in many parts of the world. They have been in regular service on the Volga River in the U.S.S.R., as water taxis in San Francisco Bay and as military riverboats.

This air-cushion "ship" has no trouble taking to the water as it skims out of its shore berth.

Handy as much smaller ACVs may be, the greatest promise for the ships-that-ride-on-air may lie in the fact that they can be made really big. There is no theoretical limit to the size of an air-cushion ship, which opens up the possibility that they could be efficiently propelled by nuclear reactors. Calculations by AEC engineers indicate that a large ship, capable of carrying 2,000 passengers, could easily accommodate a nuclear reactor and the heavy shielding it would require. They assert that, for a number of complex engineering reasons, atomic energy can be more efficiently employed in an air-cushion ship than in conventional water craft.

Such large and powerful ships might be most useful

31

Engineers lower the fuel rods into a nuclear reactor designed to power a merchant ship. Huge air-cushion ships are well adapted to powering by atomic energy.

as freighters. However, they would be so economical to operate that they could carry passengers at much lower fares than those for air travel—perhaps half the fare for transatlantic voyages. Of course, no air-cushion vehicle will ever equal the speed of the jet plane, but their economy and the luxurious accommodations that could be included aboard them lead some planners to believe that large oceangoing ACVs may have a prominent place in tomorrow's transportation picture. An air-cushion liner traveling at a speed of 150 miles an hour—not unreasonable in future craft—would make a crossing from Europe to the United States in 24 hours.

ACV liners could go right on to inland destinations.

Arthur C. Clarke, the science writer who has accurately predicted so many developments, points out: "The most shattering implications do not arise from their speed and safety, but from the fact that they can ignore the divisions between land and sea. An ocean-going air-cushion vehicle need not stop at the coastline; it can continue on inland with supreme indifference to the great harbors and seaports that have been established by 5,000 years of maritime commerce."

The greatest promise for air-cushion vehicles in the United States is in high-speed mass transit. The Department of Transportation, working with many urban and state organizations, is backing experiments that may put them to work by the mid-70s. As a high-speed train an ACV becomes a TACV—a Tracked Air-Cushion Vehicle. The first word applies to a guideway, some kind of a track which keeps the vehicle steady. At relatively slow speeds such a guide is not necessary. An air-cushion vehicle moving over land could, for example, skim above a highway. However, for travel at high speeds as a means of urban transport through congested areas, it obviously needs a definite, controlled right of way.

A monorail train in France has given a dramatic preview of TACV travel. On a 70-mile-long track from Paris to Orleans, the first 80-passenger vehicle skims along at speeds of 155 to 186 miles an hour. The wheelless, 82-foot-long car runs astride a concrete rail shaped like an inverted T. Blowers pump air into

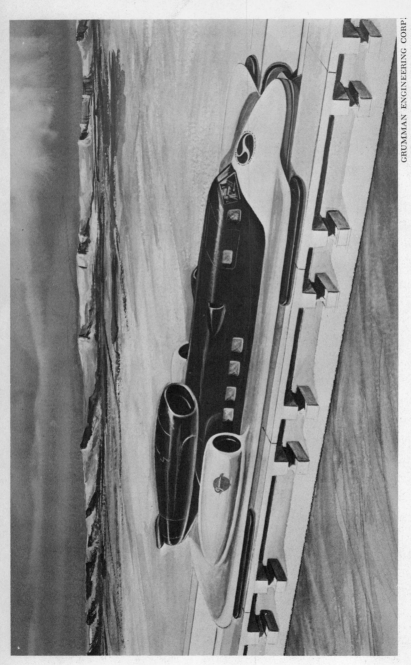

Tracked Air Cushion Vehicles may look like this artist's conception of a 300-mile-an-hour craft designed for the U.S. Department of Transportation.

A 200-mile-an-hour "Aerotrain" speeds past slow moving freeway traffic.

chambers along the bottom of the car. Rubber skirts around the outside rim of the vehicle keep the air from escaping. Although the air cushion is only about two inches thick, it still lifts the car entirely off the T-shaped rail.

Another TACV innovation is the Urbatrain, operating experimentally in Lyon, France. The vehicle hangs suspended from a hollow metal track with a slit along the bottom. Inside the track are fans which suck air into it, thus creating the cushion on which bogies (an assemblage of wheels) ride loosely. The air cushion lifts the bogies an inch off the bottom of the tube.

It is estimated that the cost of building the Urbatrain system, including the supports required for its light-weight, vibration-free cars, is only about 10 per cent of the cost of constructing subways through urban areas. Smoothness, efficiency and silence are other arguments for the suspended monorail train, which already has many points in its favor, like the fact that it can readily be placed above existent streets, freeways and railroad tracks without taking away any of the carrying capacity of these facilities.

These successful TACVs operate at much lower speeds than the models the U.S. Department of Transportation is testing at the Colorado testing grounds. One of these is capable of cruising at 300 miles an hour. It reaches this speed from a standing start in three miles and decelerates to a stop in two miles. As it goes through trial runs engineers are seeking the answers to many questions about TACV travel at such high speeds. What, for instance, would happen if a TACV, moving at 300 miles an hour, hit something that had fallen onto its guideway? Will high winds buffet it? Will it make too much noise?

While these problems are being checked out on the high-speed models, the first TACV to go into actual operation in the U.S. will begin its run on a 16-mile-long guideway in Los Angeles. It will not be the 300-mile-an-hour type, but a slower model based on the French design. However, it will reach the respectable speed of 160 miles an hour.

City planners are hopeful that as motorists crawling along clogged freeways watch it flash by, they'll get the message. They want it to show not only the automobile-oriented citizens of Los Angeles but those of the rest of the country as well that fast mass-transit vehicles are the best way to get through the urban sprawl of today's cities.

High-Speed Underground

Sometime in the 1980s you may travel on one of to-morrow's most remarkable vehicles. Let's say you're going from New York to Philadelphia. You'll start your journey in what looks like the lobby of an office build-ing, with a long row of elevator doors. As they slide open and you walk through one of them, you find yourself not in an elevator but in a car whose interior resembles that of an airliner or a rather luxurious sub-way, except that it has no windows. As you and your fellow passengers settle comfortably in the seats, the doors slide shut.

You hear a faint humming sound, so you know the train is starting. You try to detect any sensation of motion, but you feel none, even though you know that in a matter of a few seconds the vehicle you're rid-ing has shot up to a speed of over 400 miles an hour.

Soon a lighted sign flashes on at the front of the car. PHILADELPHIA—ONE MINUTE. You don't feel the train decelerating or coming to a stop, but the doors open and you step out into another lobby like the one you left in New York. You glance at your watch. Right on schedule. You've traveled 85 miles in 13 minutes.

Trains that hurtle through tunnels at airplane speeds? This is not a fanciful prediction but one based on very practical considerations. Many experts believe that the best place to put high-speed transportation systems is underground. Here noise, weather and the difficulties of acquiring right of way through congested areas present no problems.

The story of the swift, silent transportation system known as Gravity Vacuum Transit began in 1963 when a group of aeronautical engineers were handed a strange assignment. Strange, that is, for men who had always worked on airplanes and spacecraft, as had these researchers at the Lockheed Aircraft plant in Burbank, California. What could they do to apply what they had learned from aeronautics to high-speed trains for the Northeast Corridor between Boston and Washington? And perhaps, while they were at it, they could work out a rapid-transit system for metropolitan areas like New York and Los Angeles.

"We went at the job with open minds," says Lawrence Edwards, the engineer in charge of the project. "We didn't know much of anything about ground

Tube-like trains rush through deep underground tunnels in this artist's drawing of a Gravity Vacuum system.

transport, and we just had to feel our way along, thinking things through as we went."

They started with speed. Just how fast would a train have to go to really transport people at something like aircraft speeds? They decided that an average of 200 miles an hour was what they would have to try for. Counting the time lost in stops, that would call for speeds of up to 400 miles an hour between stations. Power plants to drive an aeronautically designed train that fast were available—but the idea of running at 400 miles an hour on open tracks had to be eliminated right at the start. There were too many dangers in that —ice, snow, the possibility of objects falling on the tracks. It soon became obvious that if the tracks had to

TUBE TRANSIT CORP.

Some stations on the Gravity Vacuum systems will look like this. In others the trains themselves will not be visible, but will be entered through doors that resemble those of elevators.

TUBE TRANSIT CORP.

be covered, it would be better to put them underground. That would solve the right-of-way problem
too.

Very quickly the engineers arrived at the concept of
a train hurtling through a tube from which the air had
been pumped. At this point Edwards asked a thought-
provoking question. A train that didn't have to fight air
resistance could be run by a small engine—but why
have an engine on the *train* at all? Why not use the
fixed engines that exhausted the air from the tube to
do the job? All you'd have to do to move trains through
the tube would be to keep the air pumped out in front
of them and admit air, at atmospheric pressure, behind.

The idea of driving a train by compressed air was
not new; in fact, it had already been tried out in New
York in 1870, in a one-block-long experimental subway. But Edwards went a bold step further in his
thinking. How about putting *gravity* to work to move
trains through an underground tube? Instead of building a tunnel horizontally, it could be curved in an arc,
downward from one station and upward to the next.

The train would roll downhill, propelled by gravity
and assisted by the push of air. What air remained in
the tube ahead of the train would compress in front of
it so that, as it went up the slope toward the next
station, its speed would decrease at a rate that would
finally bring it to a stop. Then the procedure would be
repeated. Once again the air pumps would remove the

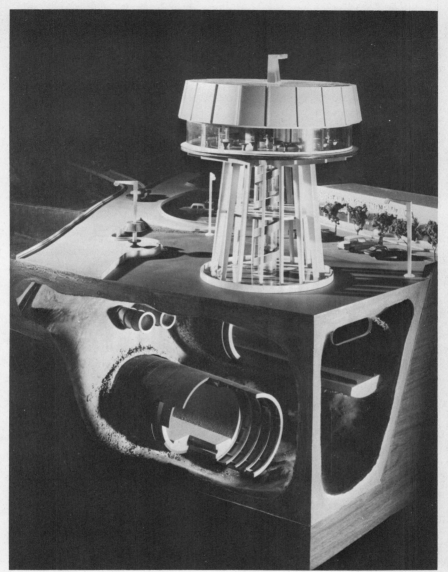

A tunnel for tomorrow—a steel tube which could be installed at any depth. Here is a way it might be used in a mass-transit system. The tower atop it is a power sub-station.

air from the tube ahead of the train, air would push it from behind and the train would be on its way.

Would such a system really work? Thousands of computerized calculations and experiments with scale models proved that it would. In one model system engineers sent a three-foot-long miniature train through a 300-foot-long tube at a speed of 230 miles an hour.

This arcing-tunnel scheme turned out to have many benefits. One was sheer efficiency, for it utilizes the principle of the pendulum. As Edwards explains: "First-year physics students learn that a pendulum, in the course of a single swing, converts potential energy (the energy stored in the suspended mass of the pendulum) into kinetic energy (the energy of the pendulum's motion) and back again into potential energy. This double conversion is accomplished with a lovely 100 per cent efficiency except for the tiny losses resulting from air drag and friction in the suspension. That is why a spring weighing two ounces can swing a four-ounce clock-pendulum weight back and forth for eight days; it would take a 300-pound spring to do the same job if the back-and-forth motion were entirely horizontal and wasted all its energy at the end of each stroke."

This efficiency could make the GVT trains very inexpensive to run. Calculations show that it would take only two dollars' worth of electricity (to run the air compressors) to move a 1,600-passenger train over a three-mile stretch between urban stations.

The biggest benefit of applying the pendulum principle, however, comes from what it can do for the comfort of the passengers. Riders on a GVT train will not feel acceleration or deceleration. The smooth descent and ascent as the train swings along the pendulumlike arc is demonstrated by a startling exhibition of how it works. On a flat car of a toy train the engineer stands an ordinary piece of chalk upright. Then he gives the car a gentle shove down a steeply sloping track. As the car accelerates swiftly down the slope, the chalk does not even wobble. It stays steady, too, as the car climbs a corresponding incline.

In a full-sized train the effect on the passengers would be the same as that on the chalk—no effect at all. For the GVT riders there would be no tendency to fall forward or backward when either sitting or standing. The surface of a glass of water on a table in a GVT car would remain unrippled, not sloshing about at all.

Detailed plans for two different GVT systems have been worked out. One would provide urban mass transit for cities such as New York. In this system the stations would be about 40 feet underground. The tunnels would dip, at their lowest points, to 900 feet —a depth which imparts a top speed of 154 miles an hour to the train as gravity draws it downward.

As the designers picture it, the trains in the system would be half a mile long. At each suburban station there would be a long parking lot directly above the train, with several access roads passing through it.

45

This would decrease local congestion and allow each passenger to park or alight from his bus near the section of the train that would put him closest to his destination. In the city, passengers would be released into a larger area than that of a conventional station, again relieving congestion.

The other plan is for an interurban system for the Northeast Corridor, although it could be adapted to other areas where cities are quite close together. Stops would be 40 miles apart, and the tunnels would dip to depths of 4,500 feet. The trains, averaging 225 miles an hour, would reach speeds of 400 miles an hour.

What are the problems that stand in the way of building GVT systems? Offhand, you might think the greatest difficulty would be the deep tunnels required. This is no problem at all, engineering studies by the Department of Transportation indicate. Deep tunnels are much cheaper to build than those nearer the surface, where water and unstable rock often create construction difficulties. The Montreal subway system tunnels, built deep in bedrock, cost only $2,000,000 a mile, less than a third the cost of the cut-and-cover type of tunnels constructed in New York. Compared with costs of surface systems, where right of way can run as high as $15,000,000 a mile, the cost of almost any tunnel is lower.

New developments, such as different ways of cutting through rock, promise to make tunnels even cheaper to build. Already in use are giant "moles,"

This experimental track is above ground but the rocket-propelled vehicles that speed along it at 5000 miles per hour give engineers valuable information about possible underground systems.

whose diamond-studded bits can literally chew their way through rock. Other methods include turning rock to dust with powerful laser beams, crumbling it with searing jets of flame and cutting it with jets of water hurled at supersonic speeds.

Gravity Vacuum Transit is not the only possible high-speed transportation system that could be operated in tunnels. Engineers have come up with many proposals that take advantage of the benefits offered by tubes. One scheme is Tubeflight, worked out by Dr. J. V. Foa of Rensselaer Polytechnic Institute. His proposal uses air propulsion to drive a car through the tube. In the Foa system air is drawn through the train by a turbojet engine and rushes out behind it, propelling the train through the tube in the same manner that a jet engine propels an airplane.

Another system, which uses a turboprop engine mounted on a 75-passenger car, was devised by students at Tufts University. Their high-speed vehicle would run on wheels until it hit a speed of 150 miles an hour. Above that speed its wheels would retract and it would become an air-cushion vehicle, moving smoothly along at speeds up to 350 miles an hour.

A scale model built by the students proved that the system would work all right as far as moving the vehicle was concerned, and the train would hurtle through the tube at the high speeds they visualized. However, the young designers discovered that unexpected headaches would be encountered in actual op-

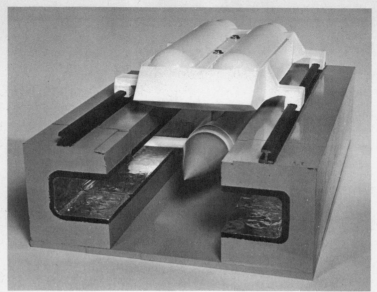

SANDIA LABORATORIES

A model of an electromagnetically propelled vehicle that may lead to high-speed underground transit systems.

eration. One of them was the problem of fumes. Deadly exhaust gases from the oil-burning engine would pollute the tube.

The solution to that, it was decided, would be to seal the car, like the pressurized cabin of an airliner, and provide the train with its own air supply. This still left the problem of keeping the fumes out of stations, where passengers would board and leave trains. Student engineers were able to solve that by an ingenious system of building the stations on turntables. The turntable would move to seal off the tubes as a train pulled in and swing out of the way when it moved out.

Experimenters are working out ways to use forces

other than air to send trains through tubes. Linear electric motors, like those proposed for air-cushion surface vehicles, might be one method. In the 2,000-foot-long scale-model experimental tube at Rensselaer, Dr. Foa and his fellow researchers are studying an unusual motive force long dreamed of by writers of science fiction—power sent by radio. Powerful transmitters would convert electricity to microwaves and broadcast these from the walls of the tube, where motors in the train would pick them up.

How soon may passengers be speeding along in high-speed underground transit systems? Perhaps the answer will come by the mid '70s, when a demonstration section of the GVT system is to be built—a 1.8-mile-long stretch in which full-sized trains will operate. Built on hill slopes, rather than underground, this huge pipe may prove that the idea of underground "pipelines for people" is not the promising solution to some of our transportation problems that many urban planners hope it is—but then again, it may mark the beginning of a new era in transportation.

◦◦◦ 4

Safer Automobiles for Tomorrow

What kind of a car will you be driving in 1980?

No one knows for sure, but it seems certain that, however the car of the future may look, it will not be powered by the kind of internal combustion engine that moves today's automobiles. For it has become widely recognized that the dependable, versatile engine that has made the automobile our most widely used means of transportation has turned out to be a menace that spews a choking cloud of poisonous gases into the air we breathe.

In 1970, the nation's automobiles poured out more than *90,000,000 tons* of pollutants. In New York City alone they produced 4,000 tons a day; in Los Angeles County more than 9,400 tons daily. Nationally, automobiles account for more than 60 per cent of the chemicals that pollute our atmosphere. In some urban areas that figure rises to an appalling 90 per cent.

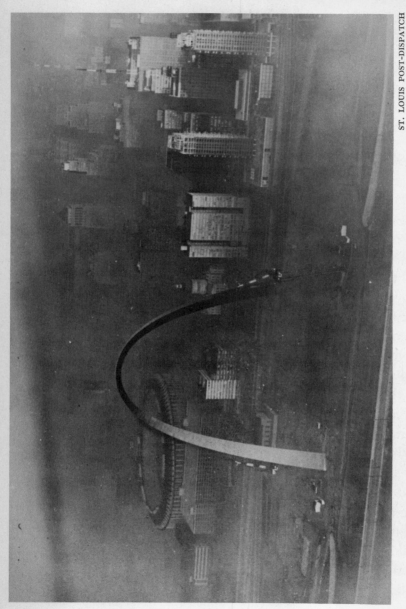

The internal-combustion engine is the chief contributor to the smog that hangs over American cities.

The chemicals given off by the internal combustion engine are some of the most dangerous ingredients in the witch's brew we call smog. One of them is carbon monoxide, a substance which interferes with the capacity of the blood to transport and release oxygen to bodily tissues. Medical authorities say that 10 parts per million in the atmosphere over an eight-hour period is the maximum amount that can be tolerated. In many urban areas, the figure runs as high as 65 parts per million, with much higher bursts during peak traffic hours.

Among other chemical culprits in exhaust fumes are the nitrogen oxides, substances which internal combustion engines produce in copious quantities. One of them, nitrogen dioxide, is toxic to people, animals and plants. In the Los Angeles area alone it accounts, every year, for more than $6,000,000 worth of damage to plants. Laboratory animals have been injured by concentrations of less than five parts per million, a quantity less than that found in some smog conditions. Chronic respiratory diseases and death have been traced to it.

Release of even one of these destructive pollutants would be reason enough to regard automobile-caused pollution as a pressing problem. Put them all together and you have what a National Academy of Sciences report calls a "national emergency."

How can we meet this emergency? The many government and industry researchers who are tackling it

53

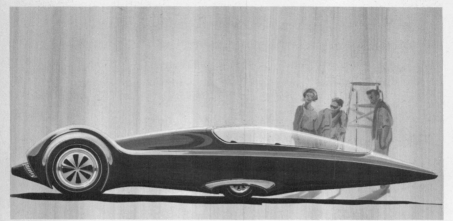

How will these possible cars of the future be powered? Certainly with engines that will not add pollutants to the air.

Can the gasoline-burning internal-combustion engine be tamed? Auto engineers like this one are experimenting with many devices to control fumes.

know that it won't be easy. To start with, the pollution fighters must reckon with the fact that the automobile isn't going to go away. There were 104,000,000 cars and trucks on U.S. roads in 1971; by 1990, there will be more than 200,000,000.

Experts all agree that the automobile will continue to be the dominant means of transportation, not only in the United States but in almost all other developed countries. Constantine Doxiadis, a noted city planner, says flatly: "Once man reaches a certain level of freedom he won't give it up, so the personal transportation vehicle is here to stay—forever." In Department of Transportation surveys in U.S. cities, over half the drivers indicated that they would continue to use their cars for commuting to work, no matter how much cheaper mass transit might prove to be.

Even the planners who are most enthusiastic about the merits of mass rapid transit concede that the automobile is needed. "Rapid transit," says a report by Cornell Aeronautical Laboratory engineers, "serves best only those people who live along the main line, and it still requires automobiles to feed it and give it a door-to-door capability."

So, with the number of vehicles on the road in the U.S. alone increasing by 3,500,000 every year, the only possible solution to the problem is to keep automobiles from giving off their noxious fumes. The first approach is to try to tame the internal combustion engine.

The automobile industry has developed various control devices which have been built into 1970 models. A passenger car with no such controls produces about 530 pounds of pollutants a year; one with them still sprays some 180 pounds of contaminants into the atmosphere.

With such devices, says Dr. John T. Middleton, head of the U.S. Air Pollution Control Commission in 1970, "we're only conducting a holding operation."

He bases this statement on the fact that any real gains are quickly wiped out by the increasing number of cars contributing their fumes to the air. A striking example of this is what has happened in Los Angeles County, which pioneered the required use of antismog equipment. By early 1969, between 75 per cent and

80 per cent of all vehicles in the area were equipped with crankcase control devices, and 25 per cent with exhaust controls.

The result? Compared with 1961, when there were no such devices, hydrocarbons in the air were reduced by only 8 per cent. To be sure, each properly equipped car was giving off fewer pollutants, but the number of vehicles had so increased that Los Angelenos were actually breathing worse air than they had inhaled in the precontrol days, when there were fewer cars.

The automobile industry is making an effort to cut out 100 per cent of the pollutants, and researchers have come up with some promising devices. One of them is a mufflerlike attachment connected to the exhaust system. It would, by a chemical process, turn the unburned chemicals into harmless carbon dioxide and water. Another device is actually a furnace that would collect exhaust gases as they left the engine and literally burn them.

Many researchers are tackling the problem from a different angle. They're working to change the gasoline. As a first step, they are removing the lead which has been added to give gasoline more power. Lead additives are a source of many of the dangerous chemicals. Automobile companies are changing engines to operate on the lower-power gasoline. Some scientists are hopeful that they can find new additives which will further reduce the pollutants.

"Why use gasoline at all?" This is the question

57

boldly asked by investigators who think they've found a fuel that will tame the internal combustion engine. It's natural gas, the same stuff that is used for home heating and cooking. When a fleet of cars in southern California was equipped experimentally with devices that permitted them to burn natural gas, the results were encouraging. They showed a 90 per cent reduction in carbon monoxide, 65 per cent in hydrocarbons and 50 per cent in oxides of nitrogen. The optimistic engineers in charge of the project believe that eventually they can come up with a pollution-free natural-gas–burning engine.

Even the most hopeful, however, admit they must hurdle a lot of obstacles. One of them is the large size required for fuel tanks. To provide enough natural gas to produce power equal to that in a tankful of gasoline requires a clumsy tank twice the size of those on today's cars. Use of liquefied natural gas would permit using much smaller tanks, but that presents the engineers with another headache. In this form natural gas must be kept in a special vacuum container that keeps it cooled to a temperature of minus 260° F.

The boldest approach of all is to forget about the internal combustion engine and find a different way to propel cars. Steam, gas turbines and electricity are three possibilities on which thousands of researchers are at work in the early 1970s.

Look at the steam car to see why some experts think that the best way to get ahead is to go back to an earlier form of automobile engine. The steam car uses an *external* combustion engine—that is, one in which the fuel is burned outside the power producing part of the engine. In it, water or other liquid is heated to the boiling point and turned into a vapor, which expands. The vapor, confined in a boiler, builds up pressure. When the pressurized vapor is piped into the cylinders of an engine it pushes on pistons which in turn rotate a crankshaft.

Why does a steam engine emit fewer pollutants? The answer is that while it still has to burn a fuel (to heat the liquid in the boiler), it burns the fuel much more completely than an internal combustion engine does. The combustion in the miniature furnace does not leave unburned portions of the fuel to be sprayed into the atmosphere.

At one time, many different makes of steam cars operated in the United States, and ever since the last Stanley Steamer was made, in 1924, many engineers have thought that steam would someday make a comeback. Today, when it looks as if this type of engine might provide a solution to the pollution problem, a number of organizations are attempting to develop steam-operated cars. The designers have encountered many difficulties in adapting a steam engine to mass production, however, and by 1971 not much progress was reported.

One company, after investing $10,000,000 in a crash program to engineer a steam car, gave up with the announcement that it could "never be developed." Later, the engineers of this concern tackled the problem afresh and backed down on this pessimistic statement. Steam enthusiasts maintain that they are well on their way toward licking the host of problems that stand in the way of mass produced steam cars—leaking boilers, the danger of explosions, the prolonged warm-up period before a steam car can be operated. Their approach has been to do away with the use of water, substituting other fast-heating liquids in closed systems.

An number of firms have produced workable one-of-a-kind models. One of them, demonstrated to a Senate Commerce Committee studying air pollution, had operated successfully for 25,000 miles. It was shown to produce only 1 per cent of the pollutants released by the internal combustion engine.

A much more likely contender to power the car of tomorrow is the gas turbine. Automobile companies have been working on this development for many years, and making turbines would better fit into the production machinery already in existence.

The basic design of a turbine is very simple. A compressor feeds compressed air into a chamber, and fuel is added and ignited by an electric spark. The hot, burning gases strike the blades of a turbine geared to the driving wheels of the vehicle. With only one spark plug, a simpler electrical system and 80 per cent fewer moving parts than today's automobile engines, the tur-

A gas turbine truck of tomorrow may help solve the fume problem on large vehicles.

bine has many advantages. It requires no oil changes and no antifreeze, and it can burn cheap fuels such as kerosene. The burning process consumes most of the pollutants, so few of them are ever exhausted into the air.

Attractive as it sounds, the turbine is not a ready-made solution to a pollution-free power plant. It is expensive to make and hard to adapt to an automobile, although it is already being widely used in buses and trucks. It may take many more years to groom the turbine for the car of the future.

What about the most-talked-of solution to the problem of pollution-producing engines—the clean, silent electric car? Why bother with gasoline, kerosene,

The Marketerr I is a pioneer electric car intended for short shopping trips. It uses less than 1¢ worth of electricity a mile, has a top speed of 25 miles an hour and a range of 50 miles between charges of its lead-acid batteries.

An all-electric bus in which the ill-smelling Diesel engine has been replaced by batteries.

steam engines, turbines or anything else? Why not let electricity drive the car of tomorrow? It may well do just that, but, like the other proposed solutions, the electric car has a formidable list of engineering hurdles to jump before it can become a common family vehicle.

The basic problem for the engineers working on the development of an electric car is the battery. The ordinary battery, which produces electric current by the chemical reaction between lead plates and sulfuric acid, is quite adequate for an automobile powered by an internal combustion engine, but it just doesn't meet the needs of an electric car. From 10 to 40 of them would be required to power an all-electric car, creating a serious weight problem.

Many new kinds of "wonder batteries" are being developed by researchers who hope to overcome the twin problems of low power and inability to hold a charge for very long. Experiments with different materials have produced some promising possibilities. One new battery, for example, uses aluminum oxide and a sulfur-sodium mixture to replace the lead-acid combination. The result is a battery with 15 times more power, capable of driving a full-sized car 200 miles at speeds of 60 miles an hour without recharging.

Various schemes have been proposed to get batteries of electric cars recharged. One is to install electric outlets in parking meters and in parking lots, so you could plug in a charger whenever you parked your car. Of course, you would do the same in your home garage

The pail-shaped container is an external-combustion Stirling engine. It charges the batteries which run this hybrid car and creates few fumes to pollute the air.

or driveway. This would serve the purpose for short runs, but it wouldn't get your car over long distances on the road. Even so-called quick charges at service stations would be too slow for the impatient motorist. So the idea of exchanging batteries has been proposed. You would drive into a service station, where a device would lift out your battery or batteries (probably more than one would be used) and substitute freshly charged ones.

Another way to solve the battery-charging problem is to provide some kind of a fuel-burning engine that will charge up the batteries while you drive, much as the battery in your present-day car is charged by a generator hooked to the engine. Several experimental

65

cars of this "hybrid" type have been built. One employs a simple external combustion engine that may be likened to a furnace. Exhaust hydrocarbons it emits are about 1/300 those sent out by an ordinary internal combustion engine. It could charge the batteries satisfactorily, but as of now the combination of the engine and the batteries needed increases the weight of a compact car by 1,000 pounds. Engineers are confident that they can find a way to beat the weight problem and make the charge-it-as-you-go electric car a reality.

The boldest approach of all to creating the electric car is to turn to a special kind of battery—the fuel cell. Fuel cells are batteries that never need recharging, because they can keep on producing electricity as long as they are supplied with fuel. They do not employ combustion in the usual sense, but create electricity by chemical reactions between two substances inside the cell. Fuel cells can operate on a variety of combinations, such as hydrogen and air, alcohol and air and propane and air.

Oddly enough, this advanced battery is really a very old discovery. Sir William Grove, an English scientist, built the first one in 1839, more than 20 years before the lead-acid battery was invented. In recent history, fuel cells have been successfully used to power equipment aboard spaceships. It was a fuel cell failure that caused the near disaster to Apollo 13. A short circuit in the tank that provided oxygen for the spacecraft's cells caused the almost fatal explosion as the

When the fuel cells that power this golf cart "grow up" they may be the ideal pollution-free method of propelling full-sized automobiles.

astronauts were on their way to the moon in 1970.

The danger of explosion is just one of the many problems confronting researchers trying to adapt fuel cells for use in automobiles. Another baffling difficulty is finding a way to make the cells give enough power without making the power package too bulky.

One model, General Motors' experimental Electrovan, has gone a long way toward this accomplishment. The engineers who designed it managed to produce perfectly safe cells small enough so they could squeeze 32 of them into the vehicle's cargo space. They produced enough electricity to operate the Electrovan for 150 miles at speeds of up to 70 miles an hour on one filling of the hydrogen and oxygen tanks.

Though still far short of what the engineers hope to accomplish, this was a long step toward the fuel-cell car they visualize as an eventual possibility. The researchers trying to develop new fuel cells are sure they will be able to make super powerful ones that will completely change the design of automobiles. They picture cells that could be built into the walls, roofs and even the doors of automobiles. The power they produced would be delivered directly to four small electric motors, each powering a wheel.

When you consider how much space is taken up by the engine in most of today's automobiles, you can see what possibilities this opens up for automobile designers. Of course, exciting as this result of fuel-cell technology might be, the big gain will lie in the ability of fuel cells to power the 100 per cent pollution-free electric car of tomorrow.

Many possible pollution-free power systems were given a try-out in the great Clean Air Race of 1970. On August 23, there was a sense of excitement on the campus of MIT in Cambridge, Massachusetts, as 39 cars lined up for the start of a 3600-mile, cross-continent contest. The cars were pitted against each other, not to see which could make the journey fastest, but which would do the least harm to the atmosphere. Although few of the automobiles looked very different from standard 1970 models, they were really quite different under their hoods.

The cars in the line-up represented a variety of power plants—regular internal combustion engines with anti-pollutant devices; turbines; electric motors; hybrid electrics. Four steam car entries were ruled out before the race because they were unable to meet the speed requirement. Students of colleges and high schools had done all the work of developing the vehicles, most of which were modified versions of standard cars provided by the auto companies cooperating in the venture.

To get a chance to enter the race, a car had to meet certain specifications. It had to be able to travel at least 60 miles at a speed of 45 miles per hour, on level terrain, without refuelling; accelerate from 0 to 45 mph in 15 seconds or less; carry at least two 170-pound people; comply with the 1970 National Bureau of Ve-

A standard automobile modified to operate on electric power. Students of Worcester Polytechnic Institute did the work that turned the hybrid electric car into a winner in its class in the Transcontinental Clean Air Car Race of 1970.

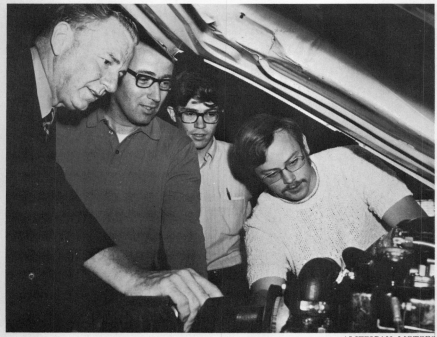

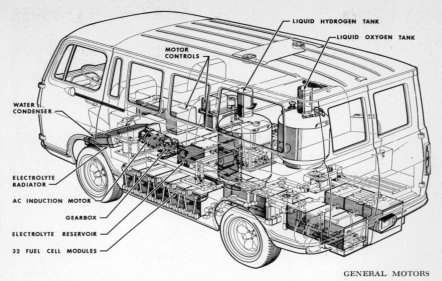

LIQUID HYDROGEN TANK

LIQUID OXYGEN TANK

MOTOR CONTROLS

WATER CONDENSER

ELECTROLYTE RADIATOR

AC INDUCTION MOTOR

GEARBOX

ELECTROLYTE RESERVOIR

32 FUEL CELL MODULES

GENERAL MOTORS

Many problems confront the designers of fuel-cell powered automobiles. One obstacle is the size of the tanks required to hold the hydrogen and oxygen.

hicle Safety Regulations; and meet the 1975 California exhaust standards for internal combustion engines.

Each day's 600-mile run was rated on elapsed time, general performance and exhaust emissions. After the race, all ratings were added up, with the most penalty points being given for the emission of pollutants. Stations along the route made exact measurements of the amount of hydrocarbons, nitrogen oxides, lead compounds, sulfur oxides, carbon monoxide, sulfuric acid and ozone emitted.

The student drivers ran into all sorts of problems arising from the kind of cars they were driving. A turbine car—actually a truck—had to keep turning off the highway at frequent intervals to find an airport where

71

it could be supplied with the jet aviation fuel it burned. The furious heat from the engine of a car burning liquid propane made the drivers so uncomfortable that they had to keep dousing themselves with cold water. Electric cars had trouble when batteries overheated.

Of the 39 entries, only 23 made it to the finish line, and only 8 of them managed to stay within the established pollutant emission limits. Since the true purpose of the Clean Air Race was to search for ways to cut pollution from automobiles, there was no great occasion for rejoicing about the results. However, the winning cars in each class did deliver some encouraging performances. Piling up the most points in its favor was a Ford Capri with a standard internal combustion engine that burned unleaded gasoline. It had several advanced emission control devices which, for part of its journey, enabled it to more than meet the 1975 California specifications. In fact, it performed well enough to meet the much tougher standards set for the nation in 1980.

Advocates of electric automobiles may have been disappointed with the performance of the all-electric cars, but a hybrid electric entry of Worcester Polytechnic Institute put on a flashing demonstration of the possibilities in this compromise vehicle. It was equipped with 20 six-volt batteries which delivered power through a conventional driveshaft. A small six-cylinder internal combustion engine constantly recharged the batteries. Pollutants from this engine were kept to a minimum by a catalytic muffler. It was not necessary to use the engine at all in cities, for the car was able to operate on power stored in the batteries. Thus this entry spread no pollutants at all in urban areas.

Actually, the fact that eight cars did make it from Cambridge, Massachusetts, to the campus of Cal Tech in Pasadena, California, within the specifications they did, proved that low-pollutant cars, having the performance today's motorists demand, can be made. Even the cars that had a hard time finishing the cross-country trek in the seven days allowed contributed something by dramatizing some of the problems that remain to be solved. In that sense there were no real losers.

As a Cal Tech student put it, "This is a race that everybody wins."

We may all be able to breathe easier in the future because of the hundreds of hours of work put in by students dedicated to doing something to help make the automobile fit to live with.

All over the world, engineers are at work on another problem that grows as the number of automobiles increases: how can cars be made safer to drive? A U.S. Government program sponsored by the Department of Transportation is aimed at slowing "the grim—and rising—tide of death and injury on the highways." This toll has been increasing at the rate of three per

73

cent a year in the United States, with almost 5,000 lives a month now being lost in auto accidents.

The designers of safer automobiles take many approaches to their task. Super powerful, fail-safe brakes; antiskid devices; warning systems that give auditory signals to remind a driver he's going too fast—these are a few possibilities. However, the main approach in creating a safer car is to find ways to better protect passengers from the hazards of collision. One scheme already embodied in an experimental car is to place the passengers in a safety capsule.

This capsule is made in such a way that, in the event of a collision, the engine, instead of being rammed into the car to crush the passengers, will be forced downward by the capsule's shape, which is like the prow of a boat. While the capsule itself is very strong, the other parts of the car are made deliberately weak. The idea is that, as they collapse, they absorb more of the energy of the collision than if they resisted it. There is that much less force left to be imparted to the capsule.

Another way of protecting the occupants of a car is to equip it with bumpers made of special energy-absorbing materials. Perhaps a design that will eventually be used will ring the car with a liquid-filled tube, similar to the water-filled bumpers already in use.

Safety car designers focus much attention on seats. In a "Survival Car" designed by Liberty Mutual Insurance Company engineers, the driver's seat is placed in the center of the car. Many accidents occur while

74

Safety car of tomorrow? A crash protection system, including a roll bar, is built into the shell of this model produced by steel engineers.

the driver is the only occupant, and in this center position he is much safer from impact on the left side than he would be if the seat were in its standard location. The seat to his right is lower than the driver's seat, to improve the driver's visibility. The bucket-type back seats are not placed directly behind the front seat positions, but are staggered so that passengers thrown forward will not be so likely to strike against front seat occupants.

Seats in a number of safety cars of tomorrow are made to protect the passenger. Bucket types have been found to be the safest, and they are made fantastically strong. Seats for one car model were built to withstand a 5,000-pound impact from any direction. Tests with mannequins in the seats showed that occupants could withstand a crash with *30 times* the force of gravity without injury when protected by these superstrength, heavily padded seats. Actual human drivers in simulated crashes were able to take even higher G forces. They were, of course, wearing seat belts and shoulder harnesses.

Seat belts and harnesses did not prove to be the safety aids it was hoped they would be. Undoubtedly they have saved many lives since they became required equipment on all new cars after 1967. The trouble is that, even in cars equipped with them, they often had no chance to help the occupants. A National Highway Safety Bureau study revealed that seat belts were ignored by 80 per cent of all drivers!

76

What is needed, safety engineers have decided, is some kind of a device that does not require the driver or passengers to take any kind of action. In the safety car of tomorrow the most promising piece of equipment is the exploding air cushion, or safety air bag.

These air bags are kept in a deflated state in a recess in the steering column, in the glove compartment and in the back of the front seat. If a car is hit with an impact equal to that of slamming into a brick wall at eight miles an hour, the bag instantly inflates. It holds the passenger behind it gently and firmly against his seat, long enough to cushion him against the shock of impact, and then deflates. The entire process, from the moment a delicate electronic sensor responds to the collision to the moment of deflation, takes less than half a second—about the time it takes you to sneeze. A passenger or driver thrown forward by the impact has moved only a few inches before he meets the inflating bag ballooning out toward him.

Used experimentally on a few 1970 automobiles, air bags are so promising that a Federal law requires that they be installed on all new automobiles manufactured in 1973 and thereafter. The safety experts believe that if the air bags had been employed on all cars involved in accidents in 1970 they would have saved at least 20,000 lives and prevented 200,000 serious injuries.

Many problems remain to be solved before the safety bags are reliable enough for universal use. One difficulty that worries the researchers working on them is noise. Might the sudden loud sound of the bag inflating injure the hearing of passengers? What about the possibility of accidental inflation? Could it actually cause an accident if a driver was suddenly distracted by the bag? Could the bag hit with enough force to hurt anybody?

Experimental models seem to have proved that these fears are groundless, but many more tests are being made by automobile makers and the companies which developed this most promising of all automobile safety devices.

Diagrams show how safety bags work to protect passengers.

1

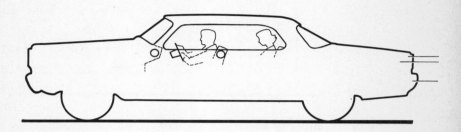

NORMAL CAR OPERATION: "Auto-Ceptor" safety pillows stowed out of sight—behind instrument panel, steering wheel hub and seat backs.

2

TIME: .00 (INSTANT OF IMPACT)

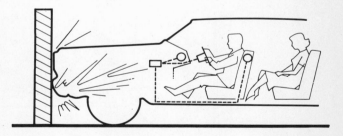

MOMENT OF IMPACT: Front of vehicle stops instantaneously; passenger compartment begins to stop, but more slowly, as vehicle front collapses. The crash sensor monitors the rate of stopping for a period of time (1 to 2% of a second) to be sure that this could only be caused by a crash.   EATON, YALE & TOWNE

3

TIME: .02 SECONDS AFTER IMPACT

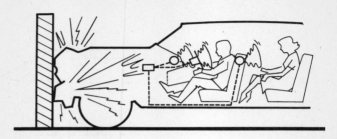

PILLOW BEGINS TO INFLATE: Sensor has signaled initiation of air supply and pillow begins to open.

4

TIME: .04 SECONDS AFTER IMPACT

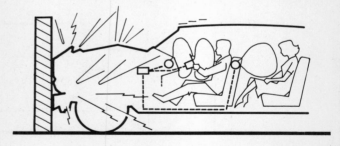

PILLOW FULLY INFLATED: 4% of a second after impact, and before occupants move forward in their seats, pillows are fully deployed and ready to stop passenger.

EATON, YALE & TOWNE

5   TIME: .06 SECONDS AFTER IMPACT

ENERGY DISSIPATION: Passenger compartment now begins to stop abruptly, pitching occupants forward into pillows. Pillows support occupants, absorb their energy and dissipate it by forcing the air through orifices.

6   TIME: .08 SECONDS AFTER IMPACT

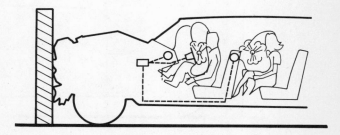

FORWARD MOTION STOPPED: Passenger compartment completely stopped. Occupants' forward motion stopped by pillows — no contact is made with interior of vehicle.

EATON, YALE & TOWNE

7 # TIME: .10 SECONDS AFTER IMPACT

OCCUPANTS' MOMENTUM REVERSED: Residual energy in pillows pushes occupants gently back into their seats.

8 # TIME: .50 SECONDS AFTER IMPACT

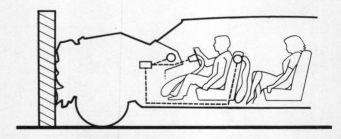

PILLOW IS DEFLATED: In .50 seconds after crash, the pillows are at zero pressure and may be easily moved out of the way for fast and easy egress from the vehicle.

∘∘∘ 5

Highways for Tomorrow

AUTOMATED EXPRESSWAY says the sign above the entrance gate. As you drive through it and up a long ramp, a red light flashes on your dashboard. A voice comes over your radio. "You are now on automatic control."

You take your hands off the wheel and your foot off the accelerator. Smoothly your car picks up speed, easing into the merging lane that runs alongside the expressway, where other cars are whizzing past at 100 miles an hour.

Magically, a place opens up for your car between the swiftly moving vehicles as they slow down just enough to keep the right distance between each one. Your car accelerates. In seconds it is racing forward at exactly the speed of the other traffic.

You relax and settle down to read a book or look at television. You know you won't have to guide your automobile in any way until it turns off at the exit you've already indicated by punching a numbered button on a special dashboard instrument. The highway has taken over the driving.

An automated highway is no far-out development of the distant future. It's a very real possibility for the near future—perhaps before 1980. Why are transportation planners considering turning over the driving to electronic controls? Not primarily to make driving easier, although it certainly does that. (Some people complain that it will take all the fun out of driving!) And, while safety is a factor—designers are sure that such highways will have *no* accidents on them—they couldn't economically consider doing it for this reason alone, important as it is.

The compelling reason for putting electronics to work on our roadways is that it seems to be the best way to solve a baffling transportation problem. To accommodate the millions of cars that will be added to already choked freeways, we must do one of two things. Either we must build more and more multiple lane roads, or we must find a way to increase the capacity of those we already have.

But look at the facts about that first alternative. The United States, which has an area of 3,600,000 square miles, already has almost one mile of road for each square mile of land! We can't just go on and on building highways, paving over more and more of our land.

Expressways, in particular, are hungry land con-

*Freeways that cut through big cities make heavy demands on
valuable urban land needed for other purposes.*

sumers. For the Interstate Highway system alone we have covered over a land area greater than that of Rhode Island. Each mile of expressway eats up 24 acres of land; a single major interchange demands 80 acres. In cities, these roads devour not only raw land but houses and business structures as well. Some 90,000 U.S. inhabitants give up their homes to highways every year.

Highways also make staggering demands on natural resources—demands which we are able to fill today but may find hard to meet tomorrow. The Bureau of Public Roads reports that enough stone to erect a wall 50 feet wide and nine feet high completely around the world at the equator went into the building of the 41,000 miles of Interstate Highways. The steel used called for extracting from the earth 30,000,000 tons of iron ore, 18,000,000 tons of coal and 6,500,000 tons of limestone. The timber needed for forms and railings denuded 4,000 square miles of forest. The drainage system took enough culvert and drain pipes to serve the water and sewer systems of *six* Chicago-sized cities.

If we try to meet our future highway needs by simply building more roadways, of the same type, we will have to construct, at the least, the equivalent of *nine more* interstate systems in the next 20 years. And many of these new expressways would soon be jammed with slow-moving traffic.

To avoid building too many new roads, and to clear

others of their traffic jams, we must find a way to make existent highway space carry more automobiles. That's where the automated highway enters the picture.

On an ordinary highway, as every driver knows, the distance between cars in any given lane must be at least one car length for every 10 miles of speed. This means that a 20-foot car, traveling at a speed of 30 miles per hour, really occupies 80 feet of highway. If this distance is maintained (and, of course, in practice, cars are often jammed up closer than that), approximately 2,000 cars an hour can move past a given point on one lane of expressway.

Offhand, it might seem that if the cars moved faster, more of them could be carried. Actually, the figure comes out very close to that 2,000 an hour, no matter what the speed of the vehicles, simply because the amount of space required between cars goes up in accordance with that formula of one car length for each 10 miles per hour of speed.

Can the space be reduced? Not without the kind of disastrous results that have occurred when a hundred or more cars have been involved in a single pile-up on a freeway.

Let electronic servants take over the driving task on a highway, the engineers reason, and you can get spectacular increases in the number of cars that can move along it. One projected automated highway would have a capacity of over 9,000 cars per hour— more than four times that of an ordinary highway.

Cars can go faster and travel much closer together when they are electronically controlled because sluggish human reaction times are no longer a factor. After you see a need to stop or slow your car, it takes about one second for the message to reach your brain, for your brain to command your foot to step on the brake and for your foot to actually do it. If you're driving at 60 miles per hour, your car will have traveled almost 90 feet before you have even started to apply the brakes. This time lag is totally eliminated by electronically actuated controls, which operate, literally, at the speed of light.

Dr. Vladimir Zworykin, the electronics pioneer, has developed a system which gives a single lane of highway a capacity of 9,000 cars an hour—more than four times the maximum number possible with manually controlled cars. There are variations of this system, but their methods of operation are basically like the Zworykin Electronic Highway.

Buried in the center of the roadway is a current-carrying cable which generates a magnetic field. As a car straddles this cable, electric coils in the car detect the strength of the magnetic field, providing indications as to whether the car is veering to the left or right of it. A small computer calculates the amount of correction needed and actuates the hydraulic device that steers the car, turning the wheels just as would a human driver. Another buried cable senses the speed of cars ahead and behind and makes the proper adjustments to the accelerator.

A highway that carries only electronically controlled cars would have the greatest capacity. However, engineers visualize combination expressways having three lanes going one way, three the other, in which the outside lanes are for manual driving, the middle lanes are transitional and the inner lanes are wholly automated.

To get into the automated system, you would first move your car from the manual lane into a transitional lane. Once in it, you would punch some buttons on a dashboard communicator which would send suitable radio messages to the controlling monitors. Your car would gradually pick up speed and be guided into a gap which would be provided by the slowing down of cars moving in the automatic lane.

To get back to manual operation, you'd simply reverse the process, punching control buttons which would move you into the transitional lane. There your car would be back in your control, and you would then move over into a manual lane as you would on any ordinary roadway.

While it sounds complicated, all the details of such a system have been worked out by General Motors, and a stretch of test roadway has demonstrated that such a combination manual and automated expressway could be made to work. Engineers estimate that it would double the capacity of an expressway at as little as one-fourth the cost of building an ordinary four-lane roadway. Their figures include the cost of the electronic equipment installed along the roadway, but not that of the receiving equipment in the automobiles. The latter would, of course, be paid for by the individual car buyers, and might cost as little as $75. per automobile.

Transportation experts cannot predict just when electronic highways will come into wide use, but they are sure that in a very few years partially automated driving will be commonplace. Several methods have already proved themselves. Among them are electronic sensing devices that measure traffic flowing along a street or road. Photo electric cells, radar or pressure plates in the roadway "count" the number of cars and transmit this information to computers, which then send out messages which turn traffic lights red or green to match traffic needs. Many cities, among them New York, Baltimore and Houston, already have some areas of computer-controlled traffic.

Applied to highways, the sensors are most useful in what traffic engineers call "ramp metering." Pile-ups at entry ramps are a main cause of traffic slowdowns on freeways. Ramp metering uses sensing apparatus that measures the flow of traffic on the roadway, feeding it to a computer which actuates traffic lights on the entry ramps. One such experimental installation on Houston's busy Gulf Freeway greatly reduced traffic snarls and increased the capacity of the highway by 10 per cent.

The Federal Highway Administration estimates that on the most heavily traveled 10,000 lane-miles of expressway there are 16,000 ramps on which metering can be used. This would increase the capacity of these roadways as much as would 2,500 additional miles of new highway, with all its demands of land, materials and money.

Another way to partly automate a highway is to use devices that send electronic messages between cars. One scheme that could be used soon is known as AHC —Automatic Headway Control. This system, which takes over all control of the car except steering, works by projecting an invisible infrared or laser beam in front of the car. When this strikes the tail lights, whether they are on or off, of a vehicle ahead, the light is reflected back to a receiver on the dashboard or under the hood. A computer then "reads" the signal and adjusts brakes and accelerator automatically so that a preset following distance will be maintained. The device works whether the car ahead has similar equipment or not.

In a system called Mini-Gap, which has already been successfully tested, the driver is free of all operating chores, including steering. Mini-Gap employs a caravan concept. Cars on a highway are linked together electronically to travel in convoys or trains. A lead car, driven by a skilled driver who handles his vehicle in a conventional manner, sends out signals to the other cars in the convoy. They follow automatically, doing just what the lead car does.

Engineers believe that it may be possible to move cars at much higher speeds than those allowable on

In the system called Automatic Headway Control a car projects an invisible beam which is reflected by the vehicle ahead of it. A computer reads the signal and sets the accelerator and brakes to maintain a safe distance between cars.

today's roadways, even without electronic automation of highways. The key to such higher speeds, they feel, is to make sure that drivers have the skills required for this type of driving. One proposal is to have rated operators' licenses, obtained after tests to determine reaction time and driving skill. Some drivers would just not qualify to drive on high-speed highways and would be restricted to other roads. To make such a rating system effective, frequent driver tests would be necessary. In many states today drivers go for years without retesting. Safety experts think that tests every six months would be desirable.

Cornell Aeronautical Laboratory researchers have taken a different approach to high-speed driving of

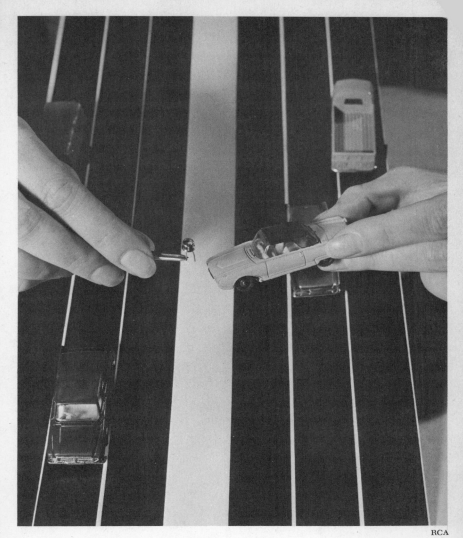

The tiny device held in the tweezers above a miniature road system is a laser, the heart of a collision warning system that may be used on tomorrow's cars. The laser sends out a beam which "bounces" off preceding cars. The beam can be used as a warning to the driver or it can actually control brakes and accelerator.

In the Mini-Gap system, cars are linked together by invisible electronic beams into highway caravans that follow a specially-built leader vehicle.

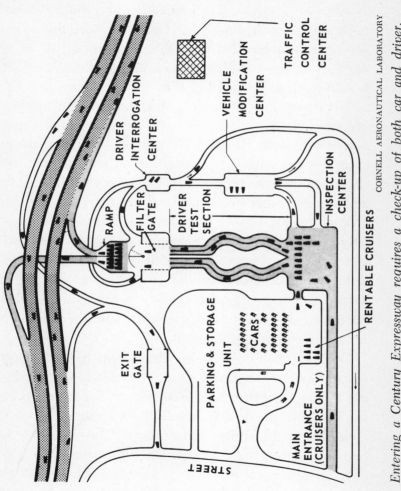

RAMP

DRIVER
INTERROGATION
CENTER

FILTER
GATE

DRIVER
TEST
SECTION

VEHICLE
MODIFICATION
CENTER

TRAFFIC
CONTROL
CENTER

INSPECTION
CENTER

EXIT
GATE

PARKING & STORAGE
UNIT

CARS

MAIN
ENTRANCE
(CRUISERS ONLY)

STREET

RENTABLE CRUISERS

CORNELL AERONAUTICAL LABORATORY

Entering a Century Expressway requires a check-up of both car and driver. Engineers of Cornell Aeronautical Laboratory have outlined a possible arrangement for a typical interchange on this 100-mile-an-hour highway.

the future. They have devised a system for frequent check-ups of drivers traveling on the CAL-designed "Century Expressway," a name based on the 100-mile-an-hour speeds which would be average for this roadway of tomorrow. To enter this highway at all, both car and driver would have to undergo a check-up. It would work something like this:

You drive up to a gateway, take out your previously obtained expressway license and insert it in a slot in a machine. As you do so, a TV camera scans your face, comparing it with the photograph on your license. At the same time, a computer is checking your license to see if there is any black mark against your driving.

You're not yet ready to go roaring out onto the highway. First you must go through the Driver Test Section. Your expressway driver's license, which required exacting tests, indicates that you're generally fit to drive on a high-speed road. But are you fit on this particular day and at this particular time? You'll have to pass two tests to prove that.

One is a steering test in which you drive through serpentine channels. You should be able to do it without having your tires hit the curb at all. Each time they do, an electronic device records the hit on a card being compiled at the "Filter Gate" ahead. The other test is one of reaction time. As you leave the steering channels, an obstacle (probably a flexible rubber device) pops up in front of you. A number of variations as to its location and nature keep you from knowing just where and when it's going to appear. How fast do you put on your brakes? Your reaction time goes down on the record waiting for you at the gate.

If you don't pass these tests, a sign will appear, or a voice speak from your radio, directing you to turn off to the Driver Interrogation Section. There an official will determine whether you have to be ruled off the highway at this time or will be allowed to retake the test.

While you've been going through your paces, so has your car, a specially designed "Century Cruiser" built for safe driving at high speeds. Electronic scanners study the condition of tires, brakes, steering and signal lights. If any vital part fails to pass the test, you will be kept off the high-speed road until the defect is repaired.

This inspection process of car and driver may sound complicated, but it would actually be completed in a few minutes. Of course, regular roadways would be available so that drivers who did not want or were not permitted to take the Century Expressway would be free to drive on the alternative routes.

The transportation planners of Cornell Aeronautical Laboratory have also worked out a system calling for the use of special compact cars called Urbmobiles. It would work like this:

You walk out of your house and get into a car that looks like an ordinary electric-powered compact. It's part of a remarkable public transportation system—the

97

The Urbmobile becomes a part of a mass-transit system when it leaves the highway and takes to the guidance tracks which carry it into the city at high speeds.

part you take home. You drive your Urbmobile down an ordinary road or street, then onto an entry ramp. That's all the driving you will do on your morning trip from suburbia to the city. Electronic controls have taken over.

They guide your Urbmobile out onto what looks like a combined railroad track and highway. Flanged wheels underneath your car let down and drop onto the tracks. A little door in the side of the car opens and a metallic arm shoots out, making contact with a power rail that delivers electricity. In a few seconds your car, no longer steered by you, is traveling at 60 miles an hour.

Thus you are whisked to your city destination. Automatically, your car is switched off onto a side track, where it glides to a stop. You step out and the driverless car moves away, headed for a parking area out of the congested heart of the city.

When you start your return trip home, there will be another car waiting there at the station for you. You will hop in and set a dial for your exit. As your car rolls off the ramp you'll take over the controls and drive it home.

The Urbmobile itself is planned as a small vehicle about 12 feet long and five feet wide. It would not go very fast—perhaps at a maximum speed of 45 miles an hour—when driven on the streets under its own power. Urbmobiles would probably not be owned by individuals but would instead be the property of an urban

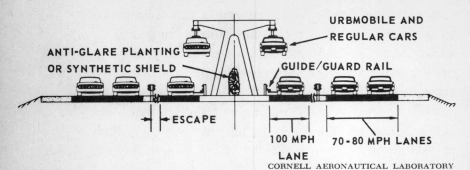

ANTI-GLARE PLANTING
OR SYNTHETIC SHIELD

URBMOBILE AND
REGULAR CARS

GUIDE/GUARD RAIL

ESCAPE

100 MPH
LANE

70 - 80 MPH LANES

Engineers planning tomorrow's transportation systems suggest this as one design for a multiple-system expressway. The suspended cars would travel at a much higher speed than the cars on the highway's surface.

transportation government agency or a private corporation running the system. The user would pay a flat sum per month for its use and, in addition, might be billed for mileage driven on the system. A credit card scanned by a machine at entrances and exits would provide a computerized record of such mileage.

There are other ways to turn cars into part of a fast-moving mass-transit system. How about a conveyor that will pick cars up and carry them suspended, somewhat like skiers on a ski lift? Cornell Aeronautical Laboratory engineers have actually devised a system like that. The conveyor would take up little room. In fact, it could be erected above the median strip of an expressway.

Another imaginative car mover is the "Glideway" system worked out by MIT engineers. They propose to load automobiles aboard tracked air-cushion vehicles which, with their 300-mile-an-hour speeds, could transport ten times as many cars as would an ordinary expressway on which they moved under their own power.

ɔɔɔ 6

Airports and Airways

A bumper-to-bumper traffic jam on all approaches to the airport . . . inside the crowded terminal a milling mob of frustrated passengers waiting for baggage . . . others lined up at ticket counters . . . on the runways, dozens of airliners, waiting for take off . . . in the air a dozen others stacked up, waiting a chance to land . . . in the towers, tired, overworked, worried controllers charged with the safety of thousands of passengers. . . .

This dismaying picture of conditions at a large metropolitan airport one day in 1970 is all too familiar to air travelers. No one who has struggled to get through a massive traffic jam, wondering all the while "Will I make it?", who has finally reached the airport only to encounter a long wait before he could get his ticket or board his plane and then perhaps found himself sitting on the runway, often for a longer time than the projected flight time to a nearby city, needs to be told that the United States is faced with a host of airport problems.

If things are bad now, what will happen when air travel soars? And soar it will. At the start of the '70s, U.S. airlines were flying one hundred billion passenger-miles a year. By 1980 this figure will climb to over three hundred billion! Much of this increase will come at metropolitan centers which are already suffering from inadequate airport and airway facilities.

We can start by finding better ways to get people to and from airports. There are many promising approaches to solving this problem, which the Department of Transportation puts at the top of the list of airport ills. A vivid demonstration of what can be done is shown by Cleveland, the first city in the United States to set up a special rapid-transit system to serve its airport.

It is 11 miles from downtown Cleveland to Hopkins Airport. This distance, short though it is, is often a nightmare of tangled traffic that can take a car as much as one hour to negotiate. With the aid of Federal funds, the city of Cleveland built a special track for electric trains that go directly into an underground station at the airport. These trains run every ten minutes on a 23-minute schedule, twice as fast as the best driving time by highway. The fare is 40c, compared to $1.60 for the limousine bus or $6.00 for a taxi. Four thousand riders a day thus get cheap, fast, trouble-free transportation to and from the airport.

While the cars on the train were built for the purpose, with special compartments to hold luggage, they

A rapid-transit system to serve airports could use cars like these to carry passengers directly to their planes.

are standard electrically powered vehicles with a maximum speed of only 60 miles an hour. Airport transportation planners visualize much faster transportation when new systems, such as gravity-vacuum or tracked air-cushion vehicles, are employed. For instance, if Dulles International Airport, which is in Virginia, 25 miles from downtown Washington, D.C., could be served by a gravity-vacuum system it would be just seven minutes away from the Capitol. To reach it at present often takes one hour or more in heavy traffic.

Planners are considering another approach to getting people to airports—taking them by air. Of course, helicopter "air taxi" service is already available at many airports, but small helicopters are expensive and not suitable for moving large numbers of people. Air buses rather than air taxis will be more practical. One scheme calls for a vehicle that looks much like an ordinary bus which would move through the downtown district picking up airline passengers at various points, such as hotels and ticket offices.

At a downtown terminal the bus would be picked up by a helicopter "Skycrane," which would carry it, its 40 or 50 passengers and their luggage to the airport. There the bus would become a land vehicle again, rolling right out to the airliner on which this particular group of passengers was going to fly. Tickets could be sold to them, or validated, and their baggage checked during the ground trip and flight to the airport. At the airliner, jacks would bring the bus up to the level of

105

Rolling "waiting rooms" take passengers directly to their planes, ending long walks and airport terminal congestion.

the plane so that the passengers could walk right in. The same method would be used in reverse to carry passengers from their jetliners to the city center air terminal or to other intermediate spots in the city or its suburbs.

Special transit systems to get people to airports easily are really a key to solving another ominous problem facing transportation planners—the need to build new airports. No matter how much existent airports are expanded, the new wave of air travel demands that many new ones be built. Take Los Angeles International Airport, for example. By 1975 it will be able to handle 30,000,000 passengers a year, twice as many as were straining its facilities in 1970. Yet, looking

This helicopter "air bus", designed for short haul inter-city routes, can carry 86 passengers at a speed of 265 miles an hour.

ahead, airport planner Francis Fox and his associates learned from their surveys that their expanded airport would fall far short of needs. It was decided that a new airport would have to be built to operate in addition to L.A. International. It would need to have a capacity of 100,000,000 passengers a year!

Where could they put the huge 100-square-mile facility they would need? You can't just plop an airport of that size down in a heavily populated area. They'd have to move it out—way out. They picked a spot in the Mohave desert, 50 miles from downtown L.A. At the same time, they laid plans for the transportation system that would enable them to choose this distant location. Tracked air-cushion vehicles, reaching speeds

107

A multiple-entrance loading system designed to get people on and off the giant jets fast.

Another design for a modern airport facility. It has unloading stations for jumbo jets as well as for smaller aircraft.

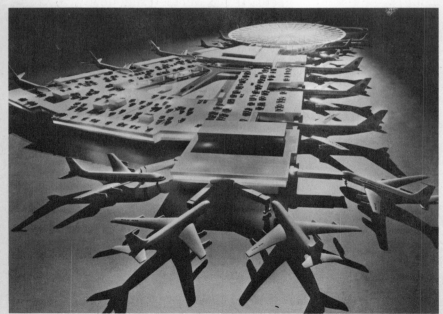

of 250 miles an hour, will, in effect, "move the airport right downtown"—at least as far as the time passengers spend getting to and from it is concerned.

Other cities are considering solving the airport transportation problem by literally bringing the airport downtown—a plan that is possible for cities located on large bodies of water. Among the cities with definite plans for putting airports on man-made islands is Chicago, whose overworked O'Hare International Airport is fast being outgrown.

Planners propose to put an 11,000-acre airport 8½ miles out in Lake Michigan, off Chicago's South Side. Engineers have calculated that it can be built by constructing an immense coffer dam in the 35-foot-deep waters of the lake. The dam would be 1,500 feet wide at the lake bottom and 50 feet wide at the top, and would rise 25 feet above the water surface. The enclosed area would be pumped dry and then filled with earth and rock or simply paved over at the lake floor level. The airport would be connected with the mainland by five miles of bridge and a tunnel at the airport end. It would take no more than 25 minutes to reach the airport by bus or automobile, less time than that by a rapid-transit system.

Probably all cities, whether near water or not, will eventually have downtown airports to provide a kind of air service that is badly needed. Why should passengers who want to fly to a nearby city have to go first to a big outlying airport at all? Why not devise a way to permit downtown-to-downtown flights?

Aeronautical engineers have discovered a way to provide such service through the development of a remarkable new kind of aircraft—the STOL (Short *Take Off* and *Landing* airplane). Many different forms of the STOL are under development. Some are able to take off in as little as 500 feet. Other related craft called VTOLs (the V stands for "vertical") can take off with no run at all. Many aircraft concerns are working to perfect airplanes of this type.

In 1970 New Yorkers got a preview of how these aircraft will operate when a pioneering STOLport went into operation. It took the form of a 100-foot-wide, 2,000-foot-long platform built atop barges anchored in the Hudson River off midtown Manhattan.

STOLcraft operating from it and other similar experimental STOLports were not large, but their basic design points the way to larger planes in the future. Within five years, optimistic airline officials predict regular STOL airbuses will be flying such city-to-city routes as Chicago–Detroit, New York–Washington, Houston–Dallas.

Helicopters may compete with, or be used instead of, the new STOLcraft. At present, large helicopters are expensive to operate and cannot achieve the high speeds of airplanes, but helicopter manufacturers are sure they can overcome these difficulties. An experimental flight from New York to Washington, in June,

110

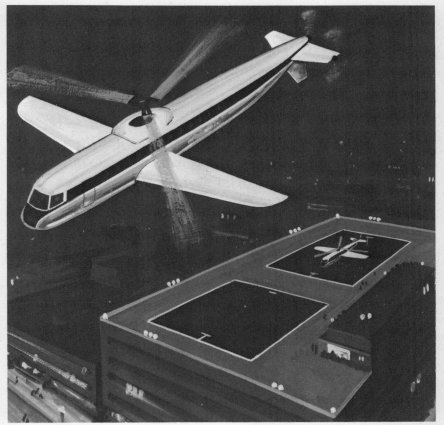

A hybrid V/STOL will be able to land on rooftops, providing downtown-to-downtown air service between cities a few hundred miles apart.

1970, demonstrated that helicopters already in existence can turn in an impressive performance. It was 9:40 A.M. when a Sikorsky helicopter with 33 passengers aboard lifted off from a heliport in the East River. One hour and 17 minutes later the big rotors were slowing to a stop as the craft landed on a lawn two miles from the nation's capitol. It was the fastest run ever made by a helicopter over that route. From downtown to downtown it represented a saving of about 45 minutes over the time needed for a passenger to get out to the airport and fly a scheduled jetliner.

The use of any kind of vertical-lift aircraft is bound to bring a change in the kind of airports. The small area required will permit building new landing facilities in downtown areas, in many instances over water or railroad tracks or on the roofs of buildings. Of course, such locations already serve as heliports in some cities, but they will become much more like full-scale airports, accommodating large numbers of passengers flying between nearby cities.

Cornell Aeronautical Laboratory researchers, in their *Metrotran* study of future transportation needs, picture a wholly new kind of downtown terminal. They see a "Master Modemixer," a huge transportation facility somewhere near the city center. The roof of the multistoried Modemixer could be a landing field for VTOLs, helicopters and air taxis. Into the lower floors of the building, much of which would be used for parking facilities and ticket offices, would flow all

112

A Master Modemixer, where all forms of transportation can converge, is here visualized as it could be built to serve Buffalo, New York.

forms of transportation—rapid-transit trains, subways, automated expressways such as those in the Urbmobile system and air-cushion ferryboats.

The picture of STOLs and helicopters landing right downtown naturally brings up the problem of noise. Won't the sound level be intolerable?

Planners relate noise at small downtown airports to the difficulty that confronts them at the big jet ports farther out. Here they are already confronted with a truly staggering noise problem. Almost all large airports today are located in congested areas, and almost all are bombarded with complaints and lawsuits about the whine and roar of jets.

Los Angeles International Airport, for instance, has been the object of *five billion* dollars in lawsuits. Hundreds of people living near the airport have sued for damages to their homes and health. A large modern school had to be abandoned because of structural hazards and conditions under which it became impossible for teachers to teach or students to study.

Fortunately, aircraft noise is not a hopeless problem. The way to attack it, in the case of both mighty jets and STOLcraft, is the same—find ways to silence engines. And that is exactly what engineers are already doing, with hope for greater advances in the future. The new jumbo jets, 747s, DC-10s and L-1011s have engines which make 25 per cent less noise than those of the smaller jet liners. The SSTs are a different story (as you will see in the next chapter), but engine designers are optimistic about reducing the noise level of all types of engines. New types of noise suppressors that use electricity to "cancel out" sound waves, now at a laboratory stage, might eventually reduce engine noise to a mere whisper.

"We *have* to find a way to cut engine noise," the chief engineer of one of the leading aeronautical companies says candidly. "No one is going to put up with the noise pollution that has been accepted in the past."

No matter what kind of an airport you start out from or end up at, you can expect that most of the troubles that plague air passengers of today will be done away with. The airlines are confident that they will be able to make air travel far more trouble-free in the future. Baggage checking, loading and unloading will be speeded up by automated, computerized conveyor systems. New methods of loading and unloading passengers from planes will get you on and off much faster. Walkways that roll into place within 30 seconds of the time a jumbo jet has taxied into its parking position are already in use at some modern terminals. All the passengers of a 747 can be off the plane in less than seven minutes, and new systems will reduce this time to three or four.

The long walks that irk weary air travelers will be eliminated at modern jetports. "People movers"— various kinds of conveyor systems, moving sidewalks and miniature electric trains—will enable you to ride where you now must walk.

115

People who arrive by automobile—and there will still be many of them, even when fast mass-transit systems are available—will find themselves able to park close to the plane they want to take or meet. Designers have projected plans for going underground, possibly building garages under the aircraft landing areas.

The happiest prospect of all for future air travelers is the end of the pile-up of planes waiting to take off and the stack-up of others waiting to land. Transportation experts base this flat prediction on the fact that the human factor is being eliminated from control of the airways. We will still have human controllers in the control towers and human pilots in the cockpits, but they will not be called upon to perform *super*-human feats.

Consider the task of the controller in today's tower. He sits before a radar screen, on which blips appear. Each of these blips represents an airplane. As the plane advances or moves away, the blip moves also. On the screen "operated" by each controller, there may be as many as 20 blips. These are the airplanes for which he has assumed responsibility. He must keep track of them and keep the pilot informed of where he should fly to avoid other aircraft or weather fronts, and how he should put his plane into a take-off or landing pattern.

When the blip appears on his screen the controller writes out information about the plane it represents on a clear plastic marker. As the plane moves, the con-

Computers will take over the tasks now carried out manually by air traffic controllers who move plastic markers representing planes across the radar display.

troller moves this marker, *by hand,* to keep it above the blip. As he does this, he also jots down on slips of paper called "flight progress strips" other flight information—like the plane's altitude, its estimated time of arrival and other data. Thus the harassed controller, who may be manipulating as many as 20 markers, is also keeping track of 20 slips, which he puts into slots alongside the radar screen.

"It's incredible! They do it all by hand!" These were the words of John Volpe, who was taken on a tour of a control tower after he assumed the office of Secretary of the Department of Transportation.

In the new automated system, which will be in use at all major airports by 1975, and long before then at

117

most of them, the hand work is eliminated. Computers on the ground monitor the aircraft continuously and move the markers, keeping them above the proper blips as they move across the radar screen. The paper flight-progress strip is done away with entirely. Instead, coded information about the plane it represents appears directly on the marker, printed there by electronic impulses from the computer. It gives the controller much more data than he could possibly jot down on the progress strips. The radar messages coded on the markers tell him not only the location and speed of the plane but also its altitude and whether it is staying level, ascending or descending.

In the future, computers aboard aircraft will provide them with a collision avoidance system independent of any help from controllers on the ground, because the computer in the airplane will monitor all nearby air traffic. This will open up more space in the skies for aircraft, since more planes will be able to fly safely in a smaller area. To provide a margin of safety today it is necessary to allow a large amount of spare space for each plane. The area taken up by a jet flying at 30,000 feet, for example, can be visualized as a huge box some 4,000 feet deep, 10 miles wide and at least 10 miles long.

Midair collisions have not occurred very often in the history of commercial aviation, but the fear of this dreaded possibility is one that today haunts ground controllers and pilots alike. In an on-board collision avoidance system, the computer makes calculations about all aircraft in the vicinity of its own plane, and warns the pilot if it "decides" there is any danger of a collision. The computer also indicates on an instrument whether the pilot should take his plane up or down or simply stay on course. If necessary, the computer can actually take over the controls and carry out the correct maneuver. The system that can do this is, of course, extremely complicated, since it must also be giving instructions to the other aircraft.

To be truly effective, the collision control equipment will have to be installed in all aircraft. The Department of Transportation predicts that by the mid-'70s this goal can be accomplished. The menace of collisions will be ended.

Air passengers of the future can expect to ride more comfortably as engineers find means to avoid another type of collision—encounters with invisible obstacles in the sky. A jet may be moving serenely through a seemingly clear sky when suddenly, with no warning, it smashes into an unseen obstacle. The plane pitches and rocks, the pilot fighting the controls. He has bumped into what has been variously described as a "blue storm," a "wall in the sky" or a "ghost tornado." Technically, the plane has encountered clear air turbulence—CAT.

This dreaded enemy of aircraft is a moving stream of turbulent air flowing in a different direction from that of other air currents. It may be a mile deep and

50 miles long, and can be traveling at speeds of 100 miles an hour or more. Unfortunately, CAT is invisible to the eye and cannot be spotted by the weather radar which enables aircraft to detect storms.

The effects of CAT on both small and large planes can be catastrophic. The force of the sudden encounter with the invisible turbulence has been great enough to tear the engines off a plane. It caused one airliner to drop 8,000 feet. A number of air crashes in the past have been attributed to it.

Long ago the French pilot Antoine de Saint-Exupéry wrote, "When you are flying very high in clear weather, the shock of a blue storm is as disturbing as if something collapsed that had been holding up your ship."

When the U.S. Air Force set up ALLCAT, a project to study this dangerous phenomenon with instruments and planes flying at different levels, it chose an ominous symbol. It depicts a ferocious jungle beast, teeth bared, about to swallow a supersonic airliner. The fact that the plane shown is an SST is significant, for CAT will be particularly menacing to these high-flying, fast-flying aircraft.

Engineers are hopeful that they can perfect a way for planes to spot CAT far enough ahead so that they'll have time to fly around it. The most promising line of attack on the blue storms is called NACATS—for North American Clear Air Turbulence Tracking System, developed by North American Rockwell. It is based on the discovery that one of the characteristics of CAT is a difference in temperature from that of the air around it. This gave the North American engineers a clue to searching it out. They developed a system which projects infrared rays from an airplane. In experimental models these have been able to sense temperature changes in the air as much as 60 miles ahead. It is hoped that their range can be extended to give the pilot of an SST a four-minute warning.

When the infrared rays hit an area of temperature difference they bounce off it and return to an instrument in the plane. This instrument feeds the data to a computer which determines the size, location and degree of turbulence and posts the information on a screen.

The combination of computerized instruments in planes and sophisticated guidance equipment on the ground will eliminate another factor that often snarls air traffic—the inability of planes to take off and land because of low visibility. When aircraft can't use a particular airport, the result is chaos. Planes stack up over the affected airport; others are held on the ground, not only at the fogged-in airport but all along the line. If New York airports are closed down, planes are held in Chicago, Denver, St. Louis and scores of other cities. Regular schedules are knocked out, and the air transport system of the whole country can be disrupted.

One day in 1969, impatient passengers at Los Angeles International Airport had a chance to witness a new way to combat a specific visibility restricter—fog.

Heavy fog blanketed the airport. Long lines of giant jets waited on the runways. In the air, arriving planes were stacked up all over southern California, hopefully awaiting some change in the fog condition that would enable them to land. The forecast did not look promising.

Then a small plane which had taken off from a fog-free airport in nearby Van Nuys roared in at 300 feet. Behind it, a path through the fog opened up. Soon the earthbound airliners were taking off, the skybound ones landing.

This method of fighting fog is an outgrowth of rain-making experiments in which clouds are seeded with chemicals to make them give up rain. When particles of certain salts are dispersed into foggy air, they absorb water and form drops of brine, which fall as rain. The problem that confronts scientists experimenting with this method of fog dispersal is to deliver the right amount of the right kind of salt at the right time.

In another approach to fog fighting, passengers and spectators at certain U.S. airports have been startled to see a strange, long-necked monster looming out of the fog. It is Fog-Sweep, a device which tackles fog from the ground instead of from the air. Fog-Sweep consists of a special truck on which is mounted a giant fan that blows air into a 100-foot-long, 38-inch-in-diameter nylon tube.

Chemicals fanned through the tube from a tank at its base are projected several hundred feet up into the

122

This strange device, called Fog Sweep, helps clear airports of fog by spraying chemicals into the air.

enveloping fog. One kind of chemical tried out by the experimenters sets up electrical charges that attract tiny droplets of fog to each other. Another kind of chemical breaks up the surface tension which ordinarily keeps the fog droplets from merging. A third chemical applies the method of the aerial attack on fog, using salt particles to make drops of brine. All approaches have the same result—heavy droplets form and fall as rain.

Of course, so-called blind landings have long been carried out with the aid of radio, radar and instruments in the plane. However, until recently these have been possible, at most airports, only under what are designated as "Category I conditions." This means that

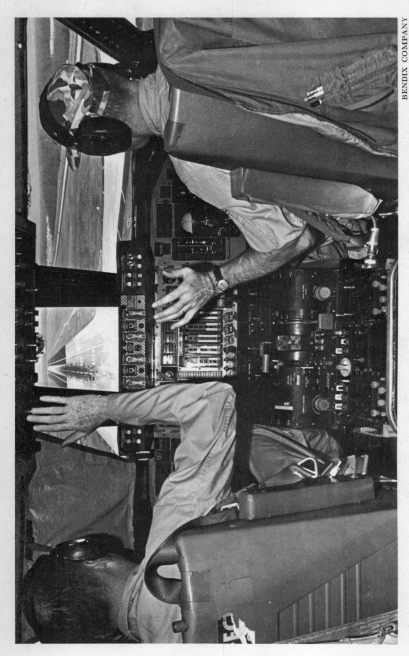

Look—no hands! Pilots demonstrate an All Weather Landing System that teams radar and computers to bring in planes when airports are socked in.

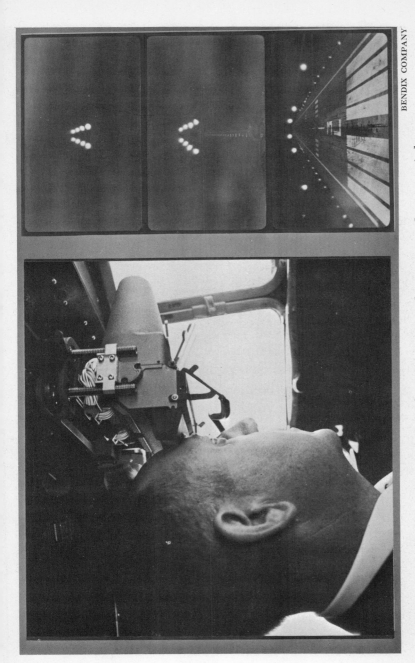

In the Micro-Vision system, the pilot "sees" radar-transmitted images of the runway lights by looking through the instrument at the left.

there is a visibility of 200 feet vertically and half a mile horizontally. In 1970, eleven U.S. airports had systems advanced enough to permit landings under Category II conditions, which are defined as having a ceiling of 100 feet with forward visibility of 1,200 feet. On a number of occasions such equipment has kept airports open that would otherwise have been closed.

The real challenge is Category III—ceiling zero, forward visibility from 700 feet to zero. Engineers have worked out several different systems for bringing airliners down safely under these "Cat Three" conditions.

A basic all weather landing system, originally developed by Bendix for the Air Force, was installed in some airliners and more than 250 military craft by 1970. In this system a computer in the aircraft keeps the plane locked on a radio beam all the way in, eventually bringing the plane's nose wheel down in exactly the center of the runway designated for landing.

Another system, called Micro Vision, uses microwave radio signals to enable the pilot to "see" through the fog. When the plane is about 10 miles from the airport, a cluster of bright spots appears on a display panel above the pilot's instrument board. These lights look just like the runway lights as they would appear on a normal clear night. Actually, what the pilot is watching is a simulation of them. Radio transmitters located alongside the runway send out signals that are received by the cockpit instrument and turned into an image.

"It's hard to believe you're not really seeing the lights directly," say pilots who have used Micro Vision.

The viewing panel is designed so that it will not interfere with the pilot's actual view of the runway and its surroundings. That is, he can be looking at the real runway, as well as he can see it under conditions of low visibility, and at the same time be watching the simulated lights that are guiding him in. Thus, even though computers are handling the landing, the pilot has the feeling of confidence and control that comes with actually looking at the runway itself.

Engineers and meteorologists are confident that, between them, they have enough weapons to win the all-weather-landing battle. They predict that soon all airports will be open 24 hours a day, every day of the year.

The SST—
Environmental
Menace?

In this book we have discussed various engineering developments that can help solve our transportation problems. Now we turn our attention to the SST, a technological achievement which, instead of solving old problems, is threatening to create distressing new ones. We *can* build supersonic airliners that hurtle through the high, thin atmosphere 15 miles above the earth at speeds up to 1,800 miles an hour—but *should* we?

This is a question that has led to the greatest controversy in the history of transportation. Ecologists, engineers, congressmen, businessmen and students are engaged in the great debate. Will the SST benefit mankind—or will it be a menace to the health, comfort and welfare of millions?

Any discussion of the SST problem must begin with

the basic reason why we need an airplane that can travel at supersonic speeds. That reason is obvious. It's fast. It will fly two and a half times faster than subsonic airliners. It will, says Najeeb Halaby, former head of the Civil Aeronautics Administration and now a prominent airline executive, "turn the Atlantic into a river and the Pacific into a lake." It will shrink the world so much that no spot on the globe will be much more than six hours away from any other.

For businessmen whose time is worth hundreds of dollars an hour, for doctors hurrying to meet some medical emergency in a distant part of the world, for diplomats hastening to deal with an international crisis, such speed could be extremely important. Fortunes and lives can indeed depend on minutes saved.

A second important reason for tackling the building of the SST is the same one that has made our venture into space pay off in many unexpected dividends—the benefit that engineers call "technological fallout." From our experience in building space hardware we have gained many new materials, such as heat-resistant ceramics, that have found uses in industry and homes. Engineers are sure we would reap many similar rewards from building the SST. They mention new heat-resistant metals, new materials for aircraft tires, new systems of aeronautical controls and many advances in aircraft engines which could be used on subsonic craft.

Three countries have already decided that these are

The world's first operating supersonic airliner is the Concorde, *built by the British and French. It flies at 1400 miles an hour.*

strong enough reasons for building the SST. England and France joined forces to build the *Concorde,* and the Soviet Union has built the Tu-144. Both of these aircraft were test flown in 1969, and may be in actual operation by 1972. The United States has spent or appropriated nearly a billion dollars to develop the early stages of an SST, the Boeing 2707, which could be in service by 1978.

Almost all major engineering problems have been solved. There is no question that the British, French, Russian and U.S. planes can all fly successfully and fast. Why then do so many people, experts and laymen alike, believe that the SSTs must never be allowed to operate in tomorrow's skies?

The case against the SST begins with the menace of

sonic boom—the sound waves that such a craft hurls earthward to batter the ground for miles on either side of its flight path. Sonic boom is caused by a sudden pressure disturbance in air. An SST literally slams into the air ahead of it, which doesn't have time to move smoothly out of the way, as air does when a slower-moving craft flies through it. As the nose of the SST violently pushes the air aside, a shock wave of this disturbed and compressed air spreads out behind the plane, in a cone shape. Some of it, seconds later, buffets the ground with what have been described as sledgehammer blows.

An SST has a bang zone (or sonic boom carpet, as engineers call it) some 50 miles or so wide. Its length is as long as the flight. In other words, if the plane flies 2,000 miles at supersonic speeds, it is creating a sonic boom carpet 50 miles wide and 2,000 miles long. All along this vast strip, people will hear and feel and in other ways be affected by the sonic boom. The greater the altitude of the plane, the wider the carpet. Weather factors, such as wind and temperature variations, can increase the width of the carpet to as much as 80 miles. Flight at lower altitudes narrows the carpet, but makes the boom within it more intense.

The most conservative estimates of the size of the area affected by an SST flying across the United States places the total carpet at 100,000 square miles—a figure arrived at by multiplying 2,000 miles (the distance the SST would fly at speeds above that of sound) by 50 (the average width of the bang zone).

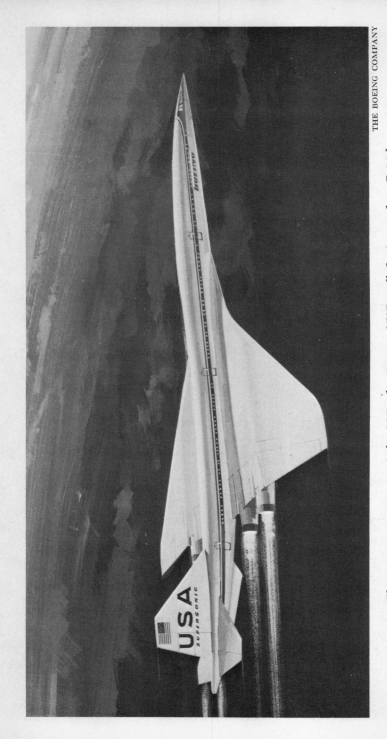

The American version of the SST—the Boeing 2707—will fly faster than British-French and Russian models. But should the U.S. build an SST at all?

The prototype of the American SST takes shape in the Boeing plant.

In Operation Heat Rise, people on the ground in many sections of the country got a preview of what may happen when a future SST flies across the country. Heat Rise (so named because of the 250° F. heat developed in the nose and leading edges of a supersonic plane) involved the cross-continent flight of a B58 Hustler bomber flying 55,000 feet high at rifle-bullet speeds of over 1,200 miles an hour.

As it sped from California to New York, millions of people were aware of its passing. In Riverside, California, plate-glass windows in a shopping center were shattered. In Colorado, people ran out of their houses, thinking they were experiencing an earthquake. Police switchboards from coast to coast were jammed as alarmed citizens reported explosions or asked bewildered questions about what was happening. Thousands wanted to sue the government for broken windows and cracked plaster, and the U.S. Air Force settled a number of claims out of court. In terms of actual dollars-and-cents' damage they did not amount to much, but the flight of the Hustler was a dismaying indication of what an SST twice as large as, and 600 miles per hour faster than, this military plane might do.

An equally disturbing discovery was made in another test, Operation Bongo, in which the citizens of Oklahoma City were deliberately subjected to a daily barrage of sonic booms. Their intensity was gradually stepped up as planes flew faster and faster. When the test ended, after 1,253 booms, the Oklahoma City *Times* ran a headline proclaiming *SILENCE IS DEAF-ENING.*

A report by the Federal Aviation Administration's SST development section indicated that, during the first eleven weeks of Operation Bongo, 90 per cent of the people stated that they could accept the eight booms that were occurring each day. At the end of six months, however, only 25 per cent felt that they could put up with such an exposure to sonic boom.

What happens to a house when it's hit by a sonic boom? Engineers have found out exactly by taking air pressure measurements. When an SST flies overhead, the air pressure around the house is normal (14.7 pounds per square inch at sea level). When the shock wave hits the house it increases the pressure of the air instantly, in 3/1,000 second to be exact. This has the effect of buffeting the house, forcefully enough to "bend" a frame house by a measurable 2/100 inch. The pressure wave enters the house, where it is reflected back and forth inside each room.

There are many situations in which a sonic boom could have a far worse effect than mere annoyance. Dr. William A. Shurcliff of Harvard University points out some of these special circumstances. Just imagine, he suggests, the possible effects of a sonic boom on a musician conducting an orchestra, or an electronic technician making a tape recording of the music; a teacher trying to hold the attention of a class; a clergyman delivering a sermon or conducting a funeral; a surgeon performing a delicate operation on a patient's eye; a horse trainer trying to calm a skittish horse, or a horseback rider following a dangerous mountain trail; a painter high up on a ladder; a fireman rescuing an invalid from a brick building, the walls of which might collapse at any time.

"To any of these persons," says Dr. Shurcliff, "a sudden sonic boom may be devastating. A boom can ruin a concert or tape recording, distract an audience or congregation, cause a surgeon's hand to jerk (and injure the patient), make a horse bolt (and throw the rider), make a man on a ladder lose his balance and fall, cause weakened walls to collapse."

SSTs will create a special menace to priceless natural wonders and historic buildings and sites. On February 21, 1968, jets of the Strategic Air Command flew over Mesa Verde National Park in southwestern Colorado. In the park, 66,000 tons of rock were loosened in rock slides that closed one of the tourist roads. Worse was the damage to the ancient Indian cave dwellings. "Several hundred caves in the area had been cracked or damaged by the supersonic flights," the park superintendent reports.

Earlier, similar effects were observed at Canyon de Chelly National Monument in Arizona. There, sonic boom loosened 80 tons of rock which crushed ancient cliff dwellings.

In Europe, sonic booms have damaged many old historic buildings. In France, for instance, the Chateau de Landal, a medieval structure, lost a tower because of the buffeting from high-flying military jets. In Germany an 18th-century abbey at Neresheim was shaken up and timbers supporting its roof weakened to the point of collapse.

In a report of the Citizens League Against the Sonic Boom, scientists connected with the organization have done some basic calculating and have emerged with some stunning figures as to just how much sonic boom damage might amount to in dollars. Assuming that the Russians put into operation 200 of their Tu-144s, the French and British 400 *Concordes,* and the U.S. 1,200 Boeing 2707s, here's the way it works out, according to the CLASB researchers:

"Suppose each of the 1,800 SSTs makes many daily trips, traveling 9,000 miles a day at supersonic speeds. This makes a total of 1,800 by 9,000, or 16,200,000 SST miles a day. Let us suppose that half of these miles—8,100,000—are over land. If the bang zone width is 50 miles, the total number of square-mile booms will be 8,100,000 by 50, or about 400,000,000.

"If, on the average, there are 100 persons per square mile (which may be typical of much of the United States in 1990), the total number of man-booms per day will be 400,000,000 by 100, or 40,000,000,000."

Since the cost in damage claims, based on past experience in Oklahoma and elsewhere, works out to $600 per million man-booms, this would bring the total damage bill to a staggering $24,000,000 a day—something like $9,000,000,000 a year!

Jumbo jets like this Boeing 747 . . .

. . . and this Lockheed 1011 . . .

. . . can carry large numbers of passengers at low cost, without presenting the environmental problems created by the SST.

What do those who favor building the SST say about the sonic boom problem? Many experts think it is being exaggerated by environmentalists. A leading spokesman for the SST, John H. Shaffer, head of the Federal Aviation Administration in 1970, says flatly, "I don't think it's even close to being the problem some opponents of the SST contend. I have heard and read speculative accounts on this subject that really amount to scare stories. Now, sonic booms have caused damage in the past, but virtually all of the 'headline' cases involved what we might call sonic boom 'accidents'— inadvertent booms by aircraft flying at low levels or engaged in military maneuvers. Some of these booms can range over 20, even up to 120, pounds per square

139

foot of overpressure, and are unquestionably severe. The boom from the SST will be far below such levels. Its boom signature at supersonic cruise will average 2 to 2.5 pounds per square foot."

Those who are against building the SST dispute Shaffer at all points, contending that the boom of the SST will be much louder than the low figures given by him and other experts. A middle-of-the-road viewpoint is that nobody—not even top authorities—really knows exactly what the problem will be. It might not be as bad as many predict—but it might be even worse.

Is there any hope of finding any kind of device that will predictably do away with the sonic boom menace? From time to time the hopes of engineers have been aroused, but as late as 1970 nothing had come of any of several schemes that might have decreased the force of the cone-shaped wave surging out behind an SST.

The only practical plan seems to be to permit supersonic speed SST flights only over unpopulated areas. This would mean that the high-speed craft would be used only for transoceanic flights. Even this, environmentalists fear, has some dangers. The battering sound waves could be destructive to marine life and damaging to ships.

Compared to the sonic boom problem, the question of ordinary noise created by the engines on take-off and landing seems almost minor. However, this is another difficulty that worries people already concerned about the noise around airports. Today's jets produce a take-off noise of 108 PNdB (perceived noise in decibels). Engineers believe the rating will be 125 PNdB or more for an SST. This may not sound like much more noise—but it is really a tremendous amount more because the units are reckoned on a logarithmic scale. Dr. Richard L. Garwin of the White House Office of Science and Technology says that an SST will produce "as much noise as the simultaneous take-off of 50 jumbo jets."

This startling prediction is disputed by other experts, such as John H. Shaffer, who believes that the SST's steep, fast take-off will actually reduce the amount of noise near an airport since it will be going on for a shorter time. Other authorities, while admitting that the SSTs will create a racket, all right, expect it to be only four times that of a jumbo jet.

Some biologists and ecologists fear another, and possibly far more dangerous, effect that the SSTs might have on our environment. Fleets of these supersonic aircraft flying through the stratosphere might actually change the climate of the world!

At low levels, the fumes from an SST's mighty engines would not emit a much greater quantity of contaminants than do the less powerful engines of subsonic jets. However, what they might do to the upper atmosphere is another matter. Here the problem is not poisonous gases but a seemingly harmless substance—water vapor.

Dr. Vincent Schaefer, Director of the Atmospheric Sciences Research Center, at Albany, New York, estimates that a fleet of 500 SSTs would dump 150,000 tons of water vapor every day. This vapor would hang suspended for years and, in cutting off sunlight, reports a Presidential committee investigating the SSTs, "would alter the radiation balance and thereby possibly affect the general circulation of atmospheric components." The blanket of moisture, they point out, could increase temperature near the ground by the "greenhouse effect" of keeping heat from being radiated back into the atmosphere.

Other scientists say that these fears are unfounded and point to recent discoveries about the atmosphere, such as the findings of Office of Naval Research Laboratory scientists. Instruments aboard balloons sent high into the atmosphere have revealed that the amount of moisture in the stratosphere has greatly increased from causes other than SSTs. In 1964 the amount of water vapor present was two parts per million of stratospheric air. In 1970 the balloon-borne instruments showed three parts per million, a 50 per cent increase. Some scientists see this as an indication that the moisture added by the SSTs would not be harmful. A fleet of 500 such aircraft would add only 7 per cent more moisture.

Another worry is that the water vapor might result in an increase of dangerous radiation from the sun reaching the earth. This might come about because, at

142

the altitudes where the water vapor would hang, it would interfere with a chemical process that takes place in the upper atmosphere which makes life on this planet possible. In this process, ordinary oxygen is turned into ozone. This ozone intercepts ultraviolet radiation which, if it reached the earth, would be damaging to life processes. Many scientists assert that the amount of exhaust from a maximum fleet of SSTs would be too minute to cause any such catastrophic results. However, the general conclusion, even of those who discount the dangers, is that "we just don't know enough to say for sure."

These are some of the elements of the controversy about the SST. There are problems other than the environmental ones that worry many people. One of them is cost in dollars. Should the U.S. Government pour billions of dollars into an SST? Up to 1970, the Government had spent nearly three quarters of a billion dollars in subsidizing the design of an SST. A Congressional appropriation of an additional quarter of a billion would push the Government's—that is, the taxpayers'—investment in the SST up to around one billion dollars before a single plane was ever built.

However, this would be only a start, for the total cost of getting an actual prototype into the air would exceed three billion dollars. Many economists figure the costs much higher—at four to eight billion. Much of this would have to come in the form of a Government loan, since private capital could not raise the immense sums required to get an SST off the ground and to finance the building of production models.

The proposal is that the funds provided by the Government be repaid as SSTs are sold. It would take a sale of 500 of the aircraft to repay the entire loan, with interest. Could that many SSTs be sold? Will the airlines really buy them, at $50,000,000 apiece? Many transportation experts believe that the airlines would lose money on SSTs, since they have less than half the passenger capacity of the jumbo jets. This means premium rates would have to be charged for SST flights, which would cut their use by tourists. Some estimates put the cost of an SST ticket at three times that for a 747 flight.

If the environmentalists are right about the effects of sonic boom, and SSTs have to be kept from flying over populated areas (a plan already agreed upon by Federal officials), such aircraft would be limited to transoceanic flights at supersonic speeds, and held to sub-sonic speeds for flights over land. This would further decrease their usefulness, and make the employment of supersonic planes by airlines even less desirable.

Those who favor the SST, even while granting that these problems exist, still believe that they should not stop the United States from going ahead with the mighty 2707. They point out that both the British-French *Concorde* and the Russian Tu-144 are actually flying. Whatever the objections to SSTs, these planes *will* be operating. Instead of the world's airlines flying American planes, as they now do, they would be flying foreign craft and the United States would lose its supremacy as the builder of passenger aircraft. Some 50,000 or more U.S. workers who would be needed to build SSTs would lose out on this particular employment. Many government officials, aeronautical experts and businessmen sincerely believe these considerations should override the theoretical environmental problems.

It is certain that if the environmental dangers created by the SST are anything like as great as the ecologists think, no one would want to subject the world to such a menace. On the other hand, if they are not real, or turn out to be much less severe than environmentalists fear, even the most determined enemy of the SST would not want to stand in the way of building the aircraft. After all, just as the slower moving subsonic jets brought the world closer together, so would an airplane that can fly at three times the speed of sound. Perhaps the optimistic forecast of Najeeb Halaby, Pan American airline executive, will yet come true:

"The supersonics are coming, as surely as tomorrow," Halaby says firmly. "You will be flying in one version or another by 1980, and trying to remember what the great debate was all about."

ᴏᴏᴏ *8*

Space Liners
for Tomorrow

The craft coming in for a landing at the big-city airport does not look much different from the other sleek jets on the runways. But there is something very special about this particular aircraft, something that puts a note of excitement in the voice coming over the loudspeakers.

"Space liner now landing. . . ."

Spacecraft that look like airplanes, and land at ordinary airports? Such a development is not some far-out, remote possibility that will be realized only in the 21st century. It promises to become a reality much sooner, for at the start of the 1970s thousands of engineers are already at work in a vast program aimed at the creation of just such a vehicle by the early 1980s.

While the problems facing these spacecraft pioneers are very different from those of engineers charged with designing systems to move people on and under the

146

ground and through the air close to the earth, their work promises to make a great contribution to tomorrow's transportation. There is much reason to believe that we will soon need to find a way to send not just a few astronauts into space, but thousands of people who will be making their journeys for purposes that will bring enormous benefits to mankind.

The people going on these space flights will not be specially trained astronauts. They will be engineers, scientists, medical doctors and, quite probably, office and factory workers. They will not travel back and forth under conditions that are hazardous or that demand physical prowess, but as safely and comfortably as they would fly in a jet today.

Stations in space will provide platforms where many activities not possible on earth can be carried out. This design for an 80-man station contains living and working quarters in the modules at the ends of the spokes.

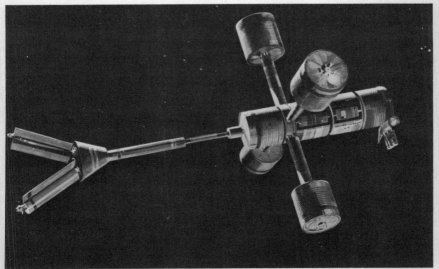

Why should we want to send all those people into space? The answer to that calls for a look at a project that promises to bring us rich practical rewards for the dollars and lives we have risked on the space effort. Well before the end of the century we are going to realize a dream long held by the space scientists. We are going to put observatories, research laboratories and hospitals in space. They'll operate aboard satellite space stations which will revolve around the earth, at a distance of 200 or more miles out. On these islands in space a variety of useful work will be performed— work that could not be done by earthbound researchers, scientists and workers.

The space stations themselves will be of varying sizes; some eventual ones will be as large as a square city block, with accommodations for hundreds of people. The first one, which the National Aeronautics and Space Administration hopes to have in orbit sometime before 1980, will be built in the 58-foot-long cylinder of a spent Saturn rocket. After this rocket has carried a spacecraft aloft, it will not be abandoned to drift uselessly in space, as is usually the case. Some of the men in the spacecraft will move into the rocket, which, with its fuel expended, will simply be a large empty cylinder, showing no trace of the liquid oxygen it carried. Partitions already in it when it left earth will provide rooms which can be used as laboratories and living quarters.

Later a much larger space station will be in orbit.

It may take the form of a huge wheel, 250 to 500 feet in diameter, as originally conceived by Dr. Wernher von Braun. There might be several tiers of rooms in the tirelike rim, which could be as thick as a three- or four-story building is high. Access from the rim to the hub, which would serve as a docking station for space ships from earth, would be provided by "spokes" in the wheel.

Centrifugal force created by the spinning of the wheel would provide a gravity effect. Any desired gravity could be achieved, depending entirely on how rapidly the wheel were rotated. It could be given full earth gravity, a half, a fourth or whatever effect was desirable for the activities being carried out in the space station. For comfort and ease of motion for day-to-day living conditions, it is believed that perhaps half earth gravity would work out best.

The cylinder and wheel design are just two of many possible forms for space stations. Another favored shape is the sphere, or rather a number of spheres hooked together by walkways. The spheres could be arranged around a hub, like that of the wheel design, and the whole assemblage rotated to provide the desired gravity. For certain purposes, a space station might consist of an unconnected cluster of cylinders, spheres or even boxlike structures.

Whatever their shape and size, the stations in space would have one thing in common: their structural parts would all be delivered by rockets, and they

149

would be assembled in space by astronauts tethered to a habitable satellite previously put into orbit.

One of the first and most obvious uses for space stations is as observatories that will give us a new view of our universe. On earth, man lives at the bottom of an ocean of air which distorts the images of stars seen through earthbound telescopes. While our atmosphere lets light through, it screens out other radiation. Some radiation emitted by stars, such as X rays and gamma rays, can't get through the atmosphere at all. Other waves, such as ultraviolet and infrared, are partially blanked out. "The astronomer," says Dr. Leo Goldberg of the Smithsonian Astrophysical Observatory, in Cambridge, Mass., "has been in the position of a reader trying to unravel the plot of a mystery novel from which most of the pages have been torn."

From the space stations far above the atmosphere, astronomers will be able to make many observations not possible from earth. Of course, unmanned satellites have already carried telescopes and other instruments into space, sending back information in the form of radio signals which are decoded and made into pictures and other readings. However, astronomers are sure that permanent space observatories, where they can look directly through telescopes and take direct readings on instruments recording radiation other than light, will permit the greatest advances in astronomy since the invention of the telescope.

NASA has developed several possible designs for

A design for a small, 12-man research station in space. Many such space platforms may be orbiting the earth in the 1980s.

space platform observatories. On one of them twelve astronomers can live and work, taking turns at a 12-inch telescope. Small though this telescope may be, it will reveal details of the heavens not shown by even the largest telescope on earth, the 200-inch giant at Mount Palomar observatory.

Along with the astronomers who head for the space stations will be medical doctors studying physiology under conditions of controlled gravity. Telemetered reports on the bodily reactions of astronauts have already provided much knowledge of the action of heart, lungs and other bodily organs in the weightless conditions of space. A space station in which the gravity could be varied for different experiments would provide an opportunity to develop much more fundamental knowledge.

Eventually, patients might be treated in hospitals in space, where the reduced gravity would place less strain on weakened hearts or other bodily organs. Of course, a strain-free means of transportation would have to be available before patients could be safely taken to a low-gravity hospital in space.

Perhaps the greatest space activity would be in manufacturing. Factories in space could make all kinds of exotic materials in zero gravity. These would include new drugs; new metals, such as a steel ten times stronger than any made on earth and alloys that cannot be made at earth gravity; and a special kind of super-glass.

Let Robert Olsen, Manager of Materials and Processes of North American Rockwell's Space Division, describe the ingenious way space glass would be made: "The oxide, mixed on earth, would be taken to the space platform and tossed into space. Then, a solar furnace, controlled from the space station, would be moved into place and its fiercely hot beam focussed on the glass materials. These would melt, floating in space as a molten glob."

After it cooled, says Olsen, "we would just go out and get it and take it home with us."

Glass thus made under gravityless conditions, and without the need for a container of any kind, will have none of the imperfections inherent in glass we now make on earth. Its purity would give it special optical qualities that would provide fantastic new lenses. Its enormous strength would make it usable for windows in high-temperature atomic reactors because it could withstand fierce heat that no other glass could take without breaking.

With so many possible uses for space stations, both the United States and the Soviet Union have made their orbiting a major space goal. To achieve it NASA engineers are faced with what they term "the most difficult project undertaken in the space program"— building a space liner that will behave like an airplane.

Of course, it would be ridiculous to try to carry any large number of people or to move any large quantity of materials by the present methods of launching and landing spacecraft. Getting astronauts off on a space voyage has always required a complicated and danger-filled blast-off. Returning them to earth by having them parachute their capsule into the ocean, where it is fished out by a Navy task force, is dangerous, uncertain and expensive. As pioneering ventures such crude methods of getting two or three astronauts at a time into space and back again were acceptable, but they won't do at all for the task of transporting tons of material and thousands of people.

NASA and aerospace company engineers have come up with a number of designs for a kind of craft that will provide space transportation on a dependable regular basis. The designs differ, but the basic principle is the same: the space liner will take off like a rocket, from facilities like those at Cape Kennedy, and return to earth as an airplane, able to land at any large airport.

One projected design for the space shuttle, which will be known officially as an ILRV—Integral Launch and Recovery Vehicle—calls for a giant craft that will weigh over 4,000,000 pounds on the ground. It consists of double fuselages, side by side. One of them is the first stage, designed to get the other one into space. This power unit is 30 feet in diameter and 200 feet long. Its twelve engines would each generate 800,000 pounds of thrust, giving the vehicle a total power greater than that of the mighty Saturn V.

As the designers see it, once this powerful set of

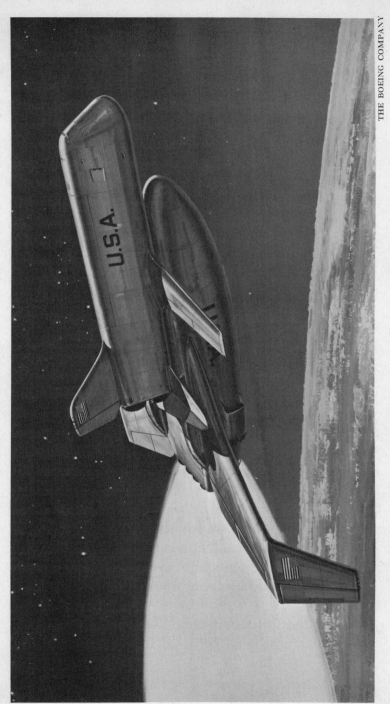

In this design for a space shuttle two vehicles have been combined. After separating at an altitude of 40 miles, the booster (bottom) would return to earth while the orbiter (top) goes on to rendezvous with the space station.

engines has lifted the two fuselages into space, they will separate. A pilot aboard the power unit will take it back to earth, while the other fuselage, which has expended little of its fuel on the take-off, continues on its way to its space station destination.

Launching of the craft will be less of a problem than re-entry. One of the earliest difficulties facing space-craft designers was what to do about the tremendous heat generated by friction with the atmosphere. The various craft that have brought astronauts home have reached a sizzling 5,000° F. This heat has been taken care of by a special insulating shroud which is partially burned up.

The shuttle craft will probably have some sort of a shroud too, possibly one which can be replaced after each journey. However, it won't have to withstand temperatures quite so great because all designs call for some easier, cooler way to enter the atmosphere. One model, it is calculated, would reach a temperature not higher than 2,000° F. It is designed to move into the atmosphere, tail foremost, its rockets slowing its progress. At 40,000 feet its nose would be tipped down and it would glide earthwards, soon reaching a subsonic speed. It would land at less than 200 miles an hour, about the landing speed of a conventional jet. In fact, some models may be equipped with auxiliary jet engines which would be used for earth landings.

Suppose you're a scientist or worker headed for a space station. What will it be like to fly into space in

156

one of the shuttle liners? After you have boarded the shuttle, you will find yourself in what looks very much like the cabin of an airliner of today. You'll settle back in your seat and fasten a seat belt and simple harness. At the moment of blast-off you will be pushed back in your seat with what engineers describe as "about the force you feel as a roller coaster car starts its descent." As the shuttle craft slowly gains speed you will have the feeling that it is not really going very fast. By the time it gets up to its 25,000-mile-an-hour escape velocity, you won't be aware of speed at all. The acceleration will be so gradual that you will never feel uncomfortable.

You will be more affected by the strange sensations produced by weightlessness. However, you'll stay strapped to your seat for the entire journey, which won't be long. It will take just a matter of minutes for the craft to reach a space station 200 or 300 miles out, although in some cases a shuttle might make a preliminary orbit of the earth. That, of course, would take an hour or so longer.

The shuttle liner trip from earth to the space station may, for some of the passengers, be the first leg of a longer journey into space—to the moon, Venus or Mars or beyond. These passengers will transfer to another craft that will be launched from the space station.

Why not blast off directly from earth? The main obstacle is the amount of thrust required to enable a

157

large rocket to break free of earth's gravity. It will be far more efficient to take parts of the long-distance rockets out to the space stations and put them together there. A ship thus assembled in space could be of any size required to accommodate men and supplies for a prolonged trip.

Craft launched from the platforms in space will use the mighty power of the atom to hurl them through the vast distances they will travel. This use of atomic energy is close to reality, thanks to the success of Project Rover, which NASA and AEC scientists and engineers have been carrying out at the Nuclear Rocket Development Station in Nevada. There, in a setting of rocks, barren mountains and stunted vegetation that looks like a scene on an alien planet, they have worked for more than 20 years to perfect a "flyable compact reactor, little larger than an office desk, that will produce more power than Hoover Dam."

At the start of the project, in the 1950s, they had a clear picture of just how they would adapt nuclear energy to space use. A conventional rocket using chemical fuels moves because of its reaction against the stream of hot, burning gases ejected from its nozzles. In a rocket propelled by atomic energy, hot gases are used in the same manner. However, the difference is that the gases are not actually burning. They are simply heated to very high temperatures by the heat fissioning atoms produce in an atomic reactor.

The combustion fuels used in conventional rockets

158

are heavy and dangerous to handle. The substances used in nuclear rockets can be much lighter. In fact, the choice of nuclear scientists as a propellant gas is the lightest of substances—hydrogen. With such an extremely lightweight propellant, a nuclear rocket can carry a much larger payload, since it does not have to expend so much of its energy just carrying fuel.

The problems faced by Project Rover scientists in developing a NERVA (Nuclear Energy Rocket Vehicle Application) engine have been formidable. There is, for example, the matter of heat. The engine must operate at a temperature three times that of earthbound reactors. In seconds after it is started up it has to go from a frigid minus 420° F. to a scorching 4,000° F. Another hurdle to jump was the design of a compact but extremely powerful pump. Its task is to deliver three tons of liquid hydrogen (compressed to 97 times atmospheric pressure) to the reactor every minute of its operation.

Even when the individual parts of the rocket system were perfected, there was still the difficulty of getting them all to work in harmony in one compact unit. Many times, in their first decade of work, the researchers were sure they had achieved success, only to find that components that worked well alone were failing as part of the system.

One of their greatest setbacks occurred when they put on the test stand an engine that, by all preliminary calculations and tests, should have been a final triumphant breakthrough. From bunkers at a safe distance they watched the plume of vented hydrogen that fanned out from the nozzles. Then they saw something ominous in the plume of superheated gas. Flashes of light—a sign of raw, uncontrolled nuclear energy. The reactor was running wild. There was nothing to do but hit the STOP button. The experiment was a failure.

Weeks later, after the "hot" engine had been dismantled by remote-control devices, they found the trouble. The liquid hydrogen rushing out at great speed had created vibrations which shook the reactor. This had made the graphite fuel elements strike against each other, causing bursts of power. It took another year and a half of work before they found a way to stop the vibration.

At the dawn of the 1970s, after many other heartbreaking failures, the Rover researchers have perfected a wieldy nuclear power packet that they call a Propulsion Module. Such a module has only 75,000 pounds of thrust, compared with the 1,500,000 pounds of the Saturn V's first stage alone, but a number of these NERVA modules can be hooked together to provide a rocket of any power desired. For the proposed Mars manned landing craft, five such modules will be used. Three will launch the rocket, a fourth will brake the craft and set it into a Mars orbit, a fifth will return it to earth orbit.

The Mars rocket dramatizes the advantages of nuclear energy. Since it will not be launched from earth, but from a space station orbiting it, the five modules give the rocket ample power. The more than 2,000,000 pounds of material that must be transported into space by successive chemical rockets to build the Mars craft is only half the amount of material required to build a chemical rocket. For long space journeys, such as that to Mars, the NERVA promises to reduce the cost of space travel by a similar amount—to less than half the cost of using chemical rockets.

Nuclear engines will transport men and machines through our solar system, but the ambitions of the space scientists don't stop there. They are busy studying forms of power that will take spacecraft into the vast reaches of space, far beyond our limited part of the galaxy.

Among the possibilities they're developing is an electrically powered rocket. It would use streams of ionized gases electrified by power from solar cells or small nuclear reactors. While such an ion rocket would have only a tiny push at any one time, it would operate continuously instead of in bursts as would other rockets. Gradually speed would build up until, after several weeks of travel, the electrical rocket would be speeding through space at 100,000 miles an hour or more.

The space scientists' dreams of space travel go beyond even this. They picture an engine that could gather its own fuel by scooping up the hydrogen atoms which exist throughout seemingly empty space. The

161

A space shuttle comes home, entering the atmosphere for the long glide into a conventional airplane landing.

A spacecraft prepares to dock at a space station which will serve as a launching platform for voyages to the moon and the planets.

hydrogen would be used as fuel for a nuclear-fusion engine and as a propellant gas which would work much as does the NERVA engine of today. A rocket thus propelled could travel vast distances. Ultimately it would travel almost as fast as light as it built up speed through year after year of its epic space voyage.

Men may never embark on such a far journey, but certainly we will soon be cruising the nearby reaches of space. Perhaps, even though you may never become an astronaut or have a job in a space station, you will be a passenger on an air liner bound away from earth.

"Space shuttles," predicts one of their designers, George Stoner of Boeing, "will someday fly families into space to view sights only astronauts see now."

Transportation for Tomorrow's World

What kind of a world will we live in tomorrow? Nobody can predict exactly, but one thing we do know for sure is that it will be a crowded world. The United States will have a population of at least 300,000,000 by the end of this century, which means that 100,000,000 more Americans will have to find places to live, work and play.

Think of it. To accommodate all these people we will need to build the equivalent of 400 cities, each with a population of a quarter of a million—or 20 cities of 5,000,000. (That's 20 present-day Chicagos!)

Of course, we will not actually build that many new cities. Most of the population will be concentrated in the giant urban sprawls that have already taken shape.

The task of moving people through the megalopolis and along the congested corridors that link one urban area to another presents a mighty challenge to transportation planners. It is not enough just to get people from one place to another; after all, today's millions somehow manage to struggle to their destinations by putting up with many irritations and discomforts. What must be provided is transportation that is much faster, more comfortable and more efficient than anything the world has known in the past.

This is a large order but, as we have seen in this book, engineers have created many remarkable devices and systems that meet these demanding specifications. If a solution to today's and tomorrow's transportation problems were simply a matter of mechanics, we could lean back with the comfortable feeling that everything was taken care of.

However, providing adequate transportation for tomorrow's millions is not basically an engineering problem. It is a *social* one, in which we are all involved, not only as passengers but as citizens. With the government playing an increasingly active role in planning transportation systems, the voters will help make the decisions about them.

Should receipts from gasoline taxes be used, not just to build highways but also to finance mass-transit systems? Should we make the operation of certain kinds of pollutant-creating cars illegal? Should we ban automobiles from certain areas and streets in our cities, turning them into malls that give priority to people? Should a government agency be set up to operate a passenger-carrying rail system to link our cities and suburbs? Should the government sponsor the building of a supersonic air transport? Should the operation of such a transport over the United States be legally forbidden? Should government funds be used to finance a vast research program in transportation?

These are just a few of the literally hundreds of questions that we all will have a responsibility to help answer. How well we do it will determine whether we can achieve that great goal for transportation in tomorrow's world—finding ways to move people safely, swiftly, quietly and economically by means that do not pollute our air or scar the face of our land.

SUGGESTED FURTHER READINGS

Aylesworth, T. G. *Traveling Into Tomorrow*. Cleveland: World Publishing Co., 1970.

Carr, D. E. *Breath of Life: The Problem of Poisoned Air*. New York: W. W. Norton & Co. (paper), 1970.

Clarke, Arthur C. *The Promise of Space*. New York: Pyramid Publications, 1969.

Commoner, Barry. *Science and Survival*. New York: Viking Press, 1970.

Davis, John. *The Concorde Affair*. Chicago: Henry Regnery Co., 1970.

Dwiggins, Don. *The SST: Here it Comes, Ready or Not*. Garden City, N.Y.: Doubleday & Co., 1968.

Hellman, Hal. *Transportation in the World of the Future*. Philadelphia: J. B. Lippincott, 1968.

Jamison, A. *Steam Cars: An Answer to Air Pollution*. Bloomington: University of Indiana Press, 1970.

Leavitt, Helen. *Superhighway—Superhoax.* Garden City, N.Y.: Doubleday & Co., 1970.

Mowbray, A. *Road to Ruin.* Philadelphia: J. B. Lippincott Co., 1969.

Ross, Frank, Jr. *Transportation of Tomorrow.* New York: Lothrop, Lee & Shepard Co., 1968.

Shurcliff, William A. *SST and Sonic Boom Handbook.* New York: Ballantine Books, 1970.

Smerk, George M. *Readings in Urban Transportation.* Bloomington: University of Indiana Press, 1968.

United Nations Department of Economic and Social Affairs. *Transport Modes and Technologies for Development.* 1970.

Von Braun, Wernher. *Space Frontier.* New York: Holt, Rinehart and Winston, 1970.

SOURCES OF INFORMATION ABOUT TRANSPORTATION

Air Transport Association
1000 Connecticut Ave. N.W.
Washington, D.C. 20036

Association of American Railroads
815 17th St. N.W.
Washington, D.C. 20006

Automobile Manufacturers Association
1712 G St. N.W.
Washington, D.C. 20006

Federal Aviation Administration
1825 Connecticut Ave. N.W.
Washington, D.C. 20009

Sources of Information About Transportation

National Aeronautics and Space Administration
Washington, D.C. 20546

National Air Pollution Control Administration
200 C Street S.W.
Washington, D.C. 20204

National Safety Council
425 N. Michigan Ave.
Chicago, Ill. 60611

Office of High Speed Ground Transportation
Federal Railroad Administration
400 Sixth St. S.W.
Washington, D.C. 20591

U.S. Atomic Energy Commission
Washington, D.C. 20545

U.S. Department of Transportation
800 Independence Ave. S.W.
Washington, D.C. 20590

Urban Mass Transportation Administration
800 Independence Ave. S.W.
Washington, D.C. 20590

ABOUT THE AUTHOR

STERLING McLEOD is a technical writer associated with a southwestern research laboratory. His interests cover a wide range of modern technology—from atomic energy to zoological research—and include, of course, high-speed mass transportation.

SCIENCE BOOK ASSOCIATES is an organization of writers and technical people active in many areas of science and technology. Their work in the preparation of audio-visual materials and training manuals to be used in science-oriented industry gives the editors an inside look at the developments that will affect tomorrow's world.